# STANDING ON
# THE SHOULDERS
# OF GIANTS

## BOOKS BY STEVEN BROOKS

*Standing on the Shoulders of Giants*

*Working With Angels:*
*Flowing with God in the Supernatural*

AVAILABLE FROM DESTINY IMAGE PUBLISHERS

# STANDING ON THE SHOULDERS OF GIANTS

The Release of Mantles to the End–Time Generation

## Steven Brooks

DESTINY IMAGE® PUBLISHERS, INC.

P.O. Box 310, Shippensburg, PA 17257-0310

*"Speaking to the Purposes of God for this Generation and for the Generations to Come."*

This book and all other Destiny Image, Revival Press, Mercy Place, Fresh Bread, Destiny Image Fiction, and Treasure House books are available at Christian bookstores and distributors worldwide.

For a U.S. bookstore nearest you, call **1–800–722–6774**.
For more information on foreign distributors, call **717–532–3040**.
Reach us on the Internet: **www.destinyimage.com**.

ISBN 10: 0-7684-2736-3
ISBN 13: 978-0-7684-2736-3

*For Worldwide Distribution, Printed in the U.S.A.*
2 3 4 5 6 7 8 9 10 11 / 12 11 10 09

# *Dedication*

This book is dedicated to every believer who, at times, has felt isolated and misunderstood by other Christians due to sovereign supernatural experiences which they have encountered from the Lord. As you read these pages, may you feel refreshed and encouraged to know that it is "normal" to live in a realm where the wonders of Heaven invade your normal, everyday life. It is my specific prayer for you that your heart be stirred continually to venture out on the Word of God beyond the elementary truths and into the deeper spiritual realities that Christ has prepared for you to walk in.

# *Acknowledgments*

I would like to express my love and appreciation to my wife, Kelly; my daughter, Abigail; and Matthew and Jennifer for your constant encouragement and inspiration. Also, I want to say "thank you" to our entire international team of ministry partners who pray for and support this ministry. Together we are working for what truly counts in the world to come.

# Table of Contents

# *Foreword*

Steven has penned another valuable work that is certain to open new doors of understanding to the Body of Christ. The subject of mantles is a topic that stirs great interest in the hearts of many diligent seekers of truth, but there has been an overall lack of material on this subject, until now.

Steven opens the Scriptures from both the Old and New Testaments to shed light on the dynamics of how mantles are given and received. The transferring of mantles has been an on-going experience from the earliest of biblical times up to the present-day Church Age. As the Lord's return draws nearer, there is an acceleration that is taking place within the Church. There is a mantling of Kingdom authority and power coming upon those with hungry and sincere hearts that will surpass any previous outpouring of God's Spirit. The Lord has saved the best wine for last. As the end-time generation stands on the shoulders of all the previous generations, there is to be expected a greater corporate vision to know and fulfill every desire within the heart of God.

As you read the pages of this book I encourage you to expect a quickening by the Holy Spirit regarding the mantle, or mantles, which God has prepared for you. Just as the Holy Spirit led me to lay my hands on Steven one day and pass on certain mantles that are upon my life, so also will the Lord find a way to equip you to fulfill your calling and purpose. The Bride of Christ is to be clothed (mantled) in white linen. The Lord's own garments of righteousness are for us to wear. As you seek Him continually, the Lord will supply every mantle, anointing, and grace needed for you to stand in the place of your intended calling. For His glory, you will be mantled to display His attributes to draw others to a deep and intimate walk in Him.

Wade Taylor
Washington, DC
Internationally recognized author and Bible teacher

# Preface

Throughout this book I have included examples of individuals whom the Lord has graciously bestowed mantles upon. By doing so I wish to express that I am not trying to promote anyone nor endorse any particular teaching. For example, I share about the Catholic saint, Padre Pio, who walked in a remarkable mantle which was later transferred to another individual. This does not mean I am in full agreement with the teachings of the Catholic church. I believe we are saved by grace through faith, and not through the doing of good works. At the same time I understand that many of the Catholic saints had a level of devotion to the Lord that far surpasses what I normally see in evangelical type churches. We (the Body of Christ) can all learn from each other as we drink from the same stream of Christ Jesus Himself. Through this book my focus and desire is to show that God is still placing mantles upon willing hearts today.

# CHAPTER 1

# *Where Are the Mantles?*

Several years back while walking through a local home improvement store, I heard a woman say in a loud voice, "Where are the mantles for the fireplaces?" The first part of this statement had a distinct supernatural ring to it that really caught my attention. In this hour, I believe God is saying, "Where are the mantles?"

Where are the mantles of great saints of old who walked in the authoritative power of the resurrected Christ and went about destroying the works of the devil? Those saints of past generations have gone on to be with the Lord, but their mantles are still available for us to reclaim and take further today. Spiritually speaking, these mantles are to be worn in "fiery places." Just as a decorative mantle often rests above a fireplace, we today can walk in mantles and see the Lord deliver us out of every fiery trial and difficulty that the devil would bring our way.

Mantles are not meant to be put on and then for an individual to go around proclaiming, "Look at me, I have Brother So and So's mantle!" You can be sure that anyone who goes around boasting that he or she has inherited some great mantle is in reality actually proving to have no true mantle from Heaven. One who has received true authority from God will walk in humility and display the love of Christ toward others. Once attained, these mantles will be of great aid and assistance to help you accomplish the work that God has for you to do in the earth. When trials and tribulations come, you will prove to be more than a conqueror because of the increased anointing of the Holy Spirit upon your life. The psalmist David said:

> But my horn you have exalted like a wild ox; I have been anointed with fresh oil (Psalm 92:10).

It's time for a fresh anointing. It's time to take the mantle that God has for you and begin to do the greater works that Jesus spoke of. Just as in the time when Elisha received the mantle of Elijah, we are now at a fork in the road concerning Church history. We must be free to move in the power of the Spirit and not be bogged down in thick religious mud. We must be free to move past basic elementary and foundational truths in the Word of God and venture on to maturity. Many churches are camped out around the simplest of Gospel truths, but they have no understanding that there is so much more to enjoy and experience. What did the writer of the book of Hebrews say?

> *Therefore let us leave the elementary teachings about Christ and go on to maturity, not laying again the foundation of repentance from acts that lead to death, and of faith in God, instruction about baptisms, the laying on of hands, the resurrection of the dead, and eternal judgment. And God permitting, we will do so* (Hebrews 6:1-3 NIV).

I read a translation one time that said, "let us get on with it." There have been times when I have sat in on church meetings and the preacher would preach a basic salvation message and share the whole redemption story all over again. I would look around the room and could easily discern that everybody in the building was already saved and born again. Then the preacher would give an altar call at the end of his message and invite any lost soul to come forward for salvation. Of course, no one came forward because everyone was already saved!

Many believers today are camped around basic Bible truths and have never moved on. If I were in school and never moved past the first grade after having been there for ten years I would become greatly concerned. Yet many times in the church, this type of spiritual lethargy is considered normal. If a person has been in the church for ten years and still does not understand simple truths such as instruction about baptisms (water baptism by immersion and baptism in the Holy Spirit with the evidence of speaking in tongues) and cannot explain these simple truths clearly to someone else, then there needs to be a renewed focus on anointed teaching to help the people of God move to the next level.

God is moving in the earth today. His Word is always the same, but God chooses to reveal Himself through fresh expressions of His grace with each generation. We should not expect Him to duplicate past revivals and previous outpourings of His Spirit. While I am sure there will be many similarities between the old moves of God and what He is now doing, we should open our hearts to receive the blessing that He has for us which will be unique, distinct, and different than what has been previously known. We need to look back for wisdom concerning previous moves of God to learn what failed and what succeeded–but we need to focus on the "now" because we can't go back, only forward.

It's a historical fact that whenever God begins to move in a fresh way, most of the opposition comes from the "old guard" that refuses to receive the new wine of God's Spirit. The "old guard" does not refer to older people, but points to those who have become settled and satisfied in their current place of spiritual mediocrity. However, there is such a hunger in the people of God today for more of His Spirit that there is no stopping or turning back regardless of the opposition. When the Spirit of God is moving, people show up. Some come out of curiosity; some out of spiritual hunger; while others come to find fault which can be found anywhere if a person looks hard enough, because we are all imperfect vessels.

New signs and wonders manifested by the Holy Spirit are coming forth. A *sign* is a directional guide that lets us know we are headed in the right direction. A *wonder* is exactly what it says it is. It is a supernatural manifestation of God's Spirit that goes beyond our mental ability to figure it out. It makes us wonder, it ignites our imagination and lifts our thoughts heavenward. As new signs and wonders flood the earth, some will say, "This is not of God." What they are really saying is that it has never happened to them. Therefore, if it has not happened to them, then it couldn't possibly be from the Lord. In whatever ways we may be misunderstood, we must still keep moving forward in love, refusing to be offended, and quick to forgive.

The Western church particularly has done all she can do to bring in the people through programs and top-notch entertainment and has only produced nominal results. But when the Spirit of God really starts moving, then it will make all the previous results pale in comparison.

Get ready, countless souls are praying and crying out for a mighty move of God. Before it's all said and done, God is going to shake this old world one more time with a mighty revival that will bring in a harvest of souls that is staggering. We must be positioned to pull in the nets from this harvest without breaking the nets. The nets represent the harvesters. The harvesters need to be fully equipped and mantled with all the backing of the Church and the angels so that there is not a collapse in dealing with the harvest.

*And when they had done this, they caught a great number of fish, and their net was breaking. So they signaled to their partners in the other boat to come and help them. And they came and filled both the boats, so that they began to sink* (Luke 5:6-7).

Many churches and ministries are not prepared for the harvest that is coming. Many people think the Lord is having a hard time bringing in the harvest. That's not the problem. The Lord is ready to bring in the harvest now, but the Church is not yet ready to handle it. If the harvest came in now I have no question that the boat would completely sink.

Recently I was asked to pray for someone who needed to receive the baptism in the Holy Spirit. I met this person and shared Scriptures from the Word to show her that the gift of the Holy Spirit is available today. I prayed for this person and led her into the baptism of the Holy Spirit. Once filled, she immediately began speaking in other tongues.

Unfortunately, as my ministry is getting busier and busier, I rarely have time to meet one on one with people to do individual teaching, and I am dismayed by how many of God's people do not know how to lead another person into salvation, water baptism, and the baptism in the Holy Spirit. The job of the five-fold ministry is to equip the saints to do these things. Time is short and the people of God must prepare for the harvest. If you are fully mantled and ready, then God can take note of that and give you a front-line role to play in His Kingdom plan.

With the release of new mantles, we will experience the cleansing fire of God and His glory. This is so greatly needed in the Church today because many saints are not conscious of the reverential fear of the Lord. There is a scriptural pattern for these types of things. When Isaiah received his commissioning as a prophet, it took place during a visionary experience in which he saw the Lord sitting on a throne, high and lifted up. Above the throne, Isaiah saw the seraphim who were proclaiming:

*Holy, holy, holy is the Lord of hosts; The whole earth is full of His glory!* (Isaiah 6:3)

The cries of the seraphim as they expressed the Lord's holiness were so powerful that it caused the posts of the door of the heavenly temple to shake. Experiencing this caused Isaiah to completely unravel as he became clearly aware of his own uncleanness. He expressed that he was a man of unclean lips (see Isa. 6:4-5), which was partially due to his being around a nation that as a whole had fallen away from God and turned to idolatry.

The overall uncleanness of the people had affected him. Isn't this true in the day and age we live in? Even if you try watching a good television program, there are those ridiculous beer commercials that come on promoting a spirit of worldliness and immorality. You may be sitting at a restaurant somewhere having a meal and the person at the table across from you has a dirty mouth that you can't help but overhear. I have noticed that usually those who talk the crudest also talk the loudest.

The challenges Isaiah faced are certainly prevalent today. The world system that is operated by satan is designed to be unholy, godless, and efficient in desensitizing those under its influence. The enemy of our souls longs to have the slime of his world system splash over on the people of God. This is why the seraphim are going to be much more active in the role of helping the end-time Church. Seraphim have six wings and they are fiery beings. Their name in Hebrew actually means *fiery ones*. What's interesting about their name is that not only are they fiery ones who burn, but their name implies they have the ability to ignite others with heavenly fire which they possess. Notice how the seraphim ministered to Isaiah:

> *Then one of the seraphim flew to me, having in his hands a live coal which he had taken with the tongs from the altar. And he touched my mouth with it, and said: "Behold, this has touched your lips; Your iniquity is taken away, And your sin purged"* (Isaiah 6:6-7).

One of the seraphim took a red-hot coal from the altar with a pair of tongs and touched it to Isaiah's lips. Just as there was a literal temple on earth that Moses, David, and Solomon erected, so is there a temple in Heaven, which is the one Moses originally copied and used as a blueprint (see Exod. 25:9). It was just after this cleansing that Isaiah was commissioned into the prophetic ministry. Many of God's people upon salvation have experienced baptism in water. Many more have experienced the baptism in the Holy Spirit. But many have no clue or understanding about the baptism in fire.

> *I indeed baptize you with water unto repentance, but He who is coming after me is mightier than I, whose sandals I*

*am not worthy to carry. He will baptize you with the Holy Spirit and fire* (Matthew 3:11).

On Sunday morning, everyone puts on his or her best. Some Christians can shout "Hallelujah!" and talk in tongues and appear to have reached the very pinnacle of spirituality. But because some have never been baptized in fire, they have no idea of what it is to live a "separated" life. This is why we have Christians today who have demon problems. Countless Christians who speak in tongues on Sunday morning and shout "Hallelujah!" were at the movie theatre the night before watching the latest horror movie that glorifies the evil spirits of death and fear. Or perhaps they were seeing the latest action show where human bodies are mutilated and profanity is spewed out by the bucket loads. Along with the violence and profanity, there is a big dose of nudity to add to the devil's slime. The Church desperately needs the fire to burn out all unholy desires to see and hear things that are spiritually impure.

## THE LACK OF HOLY SPIRIT FIRE

The lack of Holy Spirit fire is why many churches have pedophiles sitting in their assemblies. The church has become an easy target for child molesters because there is no "heat" to drive them out. The lack of heavenly flame is what allows couples that are having sex outside of marriage to sit comfortably in the pews without any repercussion. But get ready. The fire is coming back into the church! The seraphim are touching many who will be raised up as fiery revivalists who will have zero tolerance for loose living. If you think Charles Finney was a powerhouse preacher, just wait until you see his mantle fall on hundreds of fresh, men and women preachers who walk in a double portion of what he had! It's going to be glorious, and it's going to happen. A Holy Spirit inferno is coming back to the church, and those who burn with the Spirit's cleansing fire will impart the flame to others, causing spiritual forest fires to erupt wherever they go.

The seraphim will help bring the fire back into the church. Along with the seraphim will come the cherubim. The cherubim are responsible for carrying the glory of God. These are very powerful heavenly creatures that throughout earth's history have been protectors of God's glory. They are first mentioned in the book of Genesis where they were assigned to guard the tree of life after Adam and Eve were forced to leave The Garden. The tree of life had to be protected because if Adam and Eve had continued to eat of it in their sin-fallen condition, they would have prolonged their lives. It was actually the mercy of God to drive them out or else they would have continued to eat of the tree and live, while suffering endless misery in their sinful conditions.

The children of Israel apparently had a very good concept of the cherubim. When the Lord told Moses that He had chosen Bezalel as a key artisan for the work of the tabernacle, He gave detailed instructions regarding the many different tasks to be accomplished (see Exod. 3:2-11). Yet, we do not find Moses giving Bezalel any specific instructions in Exodus chapters 25 and 26 involving the exact description of the cherubim. This is because their features were common knowledge and a detailed description wasn't necessary.

Speaking of Bezalel, he was a man who walked in a special mantle that certainly needs to be reclaimed for this present age. Creative beauty and God-given genius flowed out of this man as he created exquisite designs with gold, silver, precious gems, bronze, wood, and embroidery work with yarn and fine linen. He was a master craftsman and designer in all of these different trades because the Spirit of God anointed him with wisdom, understanding, and knowledge. Bezalel's mantle is available today for those who have a similar calling and who desire to express the wonders of Heaven through their earthly artistic assignments.

## THE CHERUBIM

The cherubim are also thoroughly described in the Book of Ezekiel. When Ezekiel had his visions of God, he immediately recognized the cherubim because he had seen them repeatedly in the carved work of the outer sanctuary of Solomon's Temple. The cherubim are different from the seraphim. The cherubim have four wings, four faces, and under their wings they have hands similar to a man's. Their legs are straight and the soles of their feet are like calves feet. Their four faces consist of the face of a man, the face of a lion on the right side, the face of an ox on the left side, and the face of an eagle. The man's face on the cherubim was positioned forward and the eagle's face looked to the rear. (See Ezekiel 1:5-11.)

The cherubim on the Mercy Seat of the Ark of the Covenant looked forward, facing each other with a man's face. The early church fathers identified them with the four Gospels—Matthew the lion, Mark the ox, Luke the man, and John the eagle. The four faces represent a different aspect and quality of the Lord Jesus. The lion is the chief of the wild animals. The ox stands at the forefront of the serving animals. The eagle is the head of all that flies. Man is the highest among all of God's creation and will one day even judge angels. Ezekiel's description of the cherubim certainly doesn't fit the traditional description of a cherub as being a plump baby that shoots a tiny bow and arrow on Valentine's Day. I have no idea where some of these people come up with such silly, non-biblical ideas. Cherubs are extremely powerful and can move as fast as lightning.

The cherubim were the ones who carried away the glory from Israel. Ezekiel gives us interesting insight into what actually happened because he was not only a prophet, but a priest in the temple of Solomon as well. In Ezekiel 9:3 he speaks of how the glory of God lifted from off the cherubim that were on the Mercy Seat. The glory moved from the Ark of the Covenant to the threshold of the temple. Ezekiel chapter 10 describes how the glory leaves Israel completely. The return of the glory is not mentioned again until chapter 43 (see Ezek. 43). The cherubim are protectors and carriers of the glory of God. The cherubim are coming back to the American Church.

Sometime in the 1960s, the glory of God lifted off of the American Church to a great degree. It wasn't removed completely, but there was certainly a great loss at that time. I think an important reason for this, among several factors, was the failure of the American Church to embrace the healing revival that swept across America from 1947 through 1958. Although multitudes sat under the large tent meetings and thousands were healed by God's power, many still did not desire a deeper walk with God. Some only wanted to see a miracle. Others wanted to receive healing and then go on their way without making a deeper commitment to follow and serve the Lord.

Once when Jesus ministered on the earth, ten lepers were cleansed through His healing ministry. Only one out of the ten came back to worship the Lord.

> *So Jesus answered and said, "Were there not ten cleansed? But where are the nine? Were there not any found who returned to give glory to God except this foreigner?"* (Luke 17:17-18)

What happened after the glory lifted? Prayer was taken out of the public school system. A counter-culture of immorality, psychedelic drug use, and rock music flooded onto the scene. What many people thought was liberation was actually a deeper enslavement to the rising tide of darkness. Anarchy occurred in universities across the nation. Rebellion against any type of established authority seemed to be in style. When the glory of God was lifted off of Israel, destruction came. America has taken some pretty big hits from the enemy, but she is still standing. I believe the reason America is still standing is because there is still a core group of committed Christians that knows how to pray and knows how to stand on the Word of God. The good news, however, is that the glory of God is coming back to America! Hallelujah! The cherubim are returning and we are in for some remarkable times.

When the glory of God returns in even greater measures then ever before experienced in the American churches, it will greatly affect the landscape of the church as we now understand it to be. The glory changes everything. However, not everyone will be waiting to join the membership class, because the glory carries certain stipulations. When the glory returns, the fear of the Lord will return to the church. Today there is an enormous lack of the reverential fear of the Lord in the American Church. The glory will change that very quickly and a healthy understanding of holiness (not legalism) and separation from all that defiles will be established.

When the cherubim carry God's glory back into the American Church, we must be careful that we reverence the Lord in the beauty of holiness. King David had a very unsettling event take place in his life when dealing once with the Ark of the Covenant. He went with 30 thousand men to move the Ark from the house of Abinadab, where it had been for 50 years, to transport it to its new resting place in Jerusalem. The Ark was carried on a new cart that was pulled by oxen. As the procession moved joyfully forward, the oxen stumbled at a certain spot and Uzzah reached out his hand to steady the Ark from falling. When he touched the Ark, he was struck dead. This act of God greatly displeased David, but David realized too late that he did not move the Ark according to the rules of God's divine law. Uzzah could have been a Levite, but he was not a priest and was not allowed to touch the holy items. The Ark was supposed to be carried on the shoulders of the priests by the poles on either side of the Ark. (See Second Samuel 6:1-10.)

It's interesting that the Philistines once moved the Ark on a cart to take it back to Israel. (See First Samuel 6:8.) They were so happy to have captured it in battle, but they got much more than they bargained for. After the men began to suffer burning cancerous tumors in their rectums and a massive invasion of rats upon their land, they realized they needed to return the Ark to its rightful home, and to do so as quickly as possible! They took two milk cows and hitched them to a cart and sent the Ark back on the cart. (See First Samuel 6:1-8.)

God never dealt with the Philistines like He did with Uzzah because David and the people of Israel knew better. They knew the commands of how the Ark was to be carried. The Philistines did not know the laws of God; they were pagans outside of the covenant of God. Because of their ignorance, they were given mercy when they transported the Ark on a cart. However, as knowledgeable believers, we must understand that under a strong anointing when the glory is present, we need to be reverent in our behavior. Someone may say, "Ah well, that was under the Old Covenant. We can get by with things today because we are under grace." Yet, even under grace, we must not test the Lord. The Book of Acts, chapter 4, is not under the Old Covenant and people fell down just as dead there as Uzzah did back under the Old Covenant.

The story of Ananias and Sapphira is not about two heathens who told a lie in church and died. No, they were a married couple who were Christians that sinned under an atmosphere of a heavy glory and a strong anointing. Most likely, they saw how Barnabas was commended for selling his land and laying the money at the apostle's feet. Perhaps they wanted to be noticed and wanted recognition, so they attempted the same act by selling their land and then Ananias brought the money to Peter. What got Ananias and Sapphira into trouble was not that they did not donate the entire amount of money from their land sale. They kept some of the money for themselves and that was fine, but they lied and acted like they gave all of it. Because of this, they both died instantly for lying to the Holy Spirit. I've heard people tell lies in church many times. Why haven't they fallen down and died? Nothing has happened because of an absence of a strong presence of God's glory. However, the glory is coming back and we must prepare our hearts to stand in it. It will change the way the church is viewed by the unsaved.

> *Yet none of the rest* **dared join them,** *but the people esteemed them highly* (Acts 5:13).

The church in the Book of Acts was a church you only entered into after making an absolute commitment of devotion to the Lord Jesus. This was not a church to join in hope of finding more potential people to push the latest multilevel marketing program over on. The church in the book of Acts was a church where the fire and the glory resided. In such an atmosphere you had to be careful of your motives and actions. We desperately need this atmosphere in the churches of America today. Several years back I was visiting a church when the glory of God came into the sanctuary. I have ministered at this particular church numerous times but on this day I was not ministering, just visiting. When the glory came in, my wife and I noticed the immediate change in the atmosphere and others picked up on it as well. The worship team played softly and many of us began to feel a strong and tangible presence that seemed to cover us all like warm honey.

## NO ONE MOVED

Unfortunately, a young woman with a big, thick Bible began to walk up on the stage to give a prophetic word. I had previously seen this woman give prophetic utterances and not once was I ever uplifted by any of them. They were all soulish prophecies that didn't have the slightest bit of edification, exhortation, or encouragement to them. The local pastor should have guided her more accurately in the gifts of the Spirit but he never had the strength to correct those who were off, so they were doomed to repeat the same lifeless rituals over and over again. As she proudly and deliberately walked up the steps on the stage toward the pulpit, I thought to myself, "Oh no, not another lifeless prophecy from her again. She's going to ruin this sweet presence of the Lord that is resting upon the people."

I wouldn't dare try to correct her, because it was not my church. That was the responsibility of the pastor of that church. However, as she reached the top step she suddenly stood completely still, having been arrested by an unseen force. A weight, a glory came over her and she fell straight back on her rear-end and rolled all the way back down those steps and collapsed at the bottom in a heap. When that happened, the glory intensified among the people. God was ministering to His people and He wasn't going to let anyone get in the way!

No one moved. We all just sat there quietly for a long period of time and let the Holy Spirit minister to us one on one. It was an awesome time. Eventually, the woman who rolled down the steps slowly got up from the floor. She was dazed and disoriented, but now she was much clearer in her understanding of honoring God's presence and His glory. The glory is being carried by the cherubim back into the American Church.

Mantles are placed before us to help us move into fiery, glorious places that we are destined to walk in. Let us move forward with faith and anticipation of all He has prepared for us to experience.

# CHAPTER 2

# *What Is a Mantle?*

The word *mantle* is used to describe an outer garment worn over one's normal clothing. In Bible days, mantles were often made from an animal skin. Some mantles were used for protection from harsh weather, while others were decorated to indicate the status of the wearer. *Spiritually speaking, a mantle represents the presence and power of the Holy Spirit upon one's life.* There is no inherent power in the skin of an animal or a piece of cloth draped over the shoulders. These objects are only outward representations through which God has chosen to symbolize the power of His Holy Spirit.

Today, the Lord is still anointing His people and placing mantles upon the saints to accomplish the work He has planned for them to do. A mantle is an anointing upon you to accomplish what God has called you to do. Every born-again believer has an anointing within.

> But the anointing which you have received from Him **abides in you**, and you do not need that anyone teach you; but as the same anointing teaches you concerning all things, and is true, and is not a lie, and just as it has taught you, you will abide in Him (1 John 2:27).

As believers, we all have an anointing within that leads us into truth. The apostle John knew that this inward anointing would keep the believers from being led astray into false teaching that was put forth by the Gnostics of that day and time. The anointing within is a barrier and protection from the antichrist spirit, which is an anti-anointing that operates in the world today. The anointing within is different from the anointing upon. When the Bible mentions a mantle, it is referring to the anointing that is upon a person. A mantle was often worn over the shoulders. The shoulders speak of governmental authority.

> For to us a child is born, to us a son is given, and the **government will be on his shoulders** (Isaiah 9:6 NIV).

The anointing upon a person can be increased through quality time spent in prayer and study of the Word. A minister can be more or less anointed depending upon his or her obedience in these areas. Those called to other types of work can also increase the anointing upon their lives by walking right with God and putting their whole hearts into their work. There's never a substitute for hard work. Hard work combined with prayer and time spent in the Word will equal positive results.

I remember the time several years ago when my wife and I met Dr. Moses Cho from China when he came to California for the first time. Dr. Cho had escaped from China while having been on the "most wanted" list for counter revolutionary activity. That simply meant he started a bunch of underground churches and the government was against any form of Christian evangelism.

Now in his '70s, Brother Moses has labored many decades throughout China and East Asia, having surpassed the mark of having planted over 3,000 churches. As we talked and spent time together, he shared with my wife and me about his many narrow escapes from the Chinese army through angelic intervention. We rejoiced as he talked about the time he was being pursued by an entire convoy of army jeeps. The soldiers were desperately trying to catch him and were extremely aggravated at the many times he had slipped through their fingers. Despite driving as fast as he could, the army was quickly catching up with him when Brother Moses drove across a narrow one-lane mountain bridge that only had enough room for a single vehicle. As soon as he crossed the bridge he looked back to see the convoy race onto the bridge at full speed. Suddenly the lead jeep in the convoy blew out the front right tire and swerved into the side of the railing, being firmly wedged into the side of the metal bridge and unable to be moved. The entire army convoy piled up in a long line as Brother Moses kept the pedal to the metal and disappeared out of their sight, having escaped again from an entire army.

## WALKING IN AN APOSTOLIC MANTLE

When it comes to walking in an apostolic mantle, I'll never forget when Kelly and I went out to eat at a large Chinese restaurant in Orange County, California with Brother Moses. Please understand that Brother Moses himself owns five large restaurants outside of China in other Asian countries. One of his restaurants can seat one thousand people and it's packed for lunch everyday. He uses his restaurants as a primary means of supplying funds to the many churches that he starts. Whenever he sends out a pastor to start a church, he is able to financially support that pastor through the great success that the Lord has given to his restaurant business. Brother Moses not only knows the Lord very well, but he also knows good food when he sees it.

That day as Kelly and I walked into the Chinese restaurant with Brother Moses, it was amazing to see the instant reaction that took place when the Chinese-American workers saw him. They immediately ran to the back to inform the head chef of a "guest" arrival. The head chef hurried out and began instructing that the very best seafood be brought out to the buffet table. Workers frantically began working on the salad bar to make it look perfect. It seemed as if they were all vying for the approval of Brother Moses. Why were they doing this? It was not because they knew him; they had never seen him before. They recognized something upon him that drew a response. It was that mantle of being a restaurant tycoon that somehow was communicated without a word being spoken. When there is a strong mantle, people can sense the anointing you carry, even if they can't quite put their finger on what it is.

## ANOINTING FOR YOUR SPHERE OF INFLUENCE

The anointing is there for you to operate in the sphere of influence that God has given to you. For Brother Moses, it was an apostolic ministry combined with a large restaurant business. That is where the realm of his anointing operates. I'm sure Brother Moses would not have gotten the same response if he had walked into a skateboard shop. There he would have been out of his sphere of influence. The apostle Paul understood this principle as well.

> *We, however, will not boast beyond measure, **but within the limits of the sphere which God appointed us**—a sphere which especially includes you* (2 Corinthians 10:13).

We all have a circle of influence where we have the opportunity to make an impact with the Gospel. Some people are in the wrong sphere and need to move into the place where they can be effective with the particular anointing they carry. When I ran track in college, there was a friend of mine who loved running. He tried out for the track team, but didn't make it. Yet, he wanted to be a successful distance runner so much that he still would run with us every day. However, he was a hopeless cause as a runner. It seemed that with running, nothing ever came together for him. His form of running was awkward and clumsy. Even after several years of collegiate training he still couldn't break a five-minute mile.

One time, he purchased the most expensive pair of running shoes available, but on our long run that day, his air cushion compartment in his new shoe somehow got punctured and he appeared to be running like someone with a flat tire. Nothing with running seemed to work for him.

One evening after dinner, my friend and I went to a Christian devotional on the grounds of the Christian university we attended. There were about 300 college students gathered together singing devotional songs. My friend and I sat down toward the rear of the group because the singing had already started. Now this was simply a cappella singing going on, which is music with no accompanying instruments. It was beautiful to hear as the four part harmonies merged. My friend and I just jumped right in and started singing along with the group. However, when he opened his mouth and began to sing, I couldn't believe it. He had a voice like an angel. Suddenly, people began to turn around to see where the rich, beautiful baritone voice was coming from. There were a lot of people there, but he stood out from the whole group. As people kept looking back, I was hoping they thought it was me! But his gift couldn't be hidden. I said to him, "You never told me you could sing like that! You don't need to be on the track team, you need to go join the choir and not hide this gift."

Praise God! Some people are working the wrong job or living in the wrong place and they wonder why nothing seems to work for them. Get in your sphere of anointing and allow God to flow through you to be a blessing to others.

Jesus understood the anointing that was upon Him. There is nothing wrong with knowing you are anointed. Some people display a false humility and pretend they are no good at anything in life.

I have a good friend who is a senior technician with Audi automotive. He can fix any problem with any Audi car that exists. Even the twin turbo versions that are very complex to work on are no problem for him. He makes good money and deserves to be paid well because he is anointed by God to do what he does. If you owned an Audi car with an engine problem and came to the dealership that he works at he would without a doubt fix your car. He wouldn't display false pride and say, "I'll do my best but I'm not sure if I can do it." No, he has confidence in who he is in the Lord. He would hook your car up to the computer and run his diagnostic tests, then pull out his tools and go to work. In no time he'd have you back on the road again. Many of my friend's coworkers marvel at his ability to quickly solve technical problems on Audi cars and how he consistently overcomes every vehicle problem.

Jesus also knew God's plan for His life and exercised the anointing that He carried.

*The Spirit of the Lord is **upon** Me, because **He has anointed Me**...*(Luke 4:18).

In this passage of Scripture, Jesus was quoting from Isaiah chapter 61 (see Isa. 61:1). After He finished reading, He rolled up the scroll and handed it back to the attendant. He then sat down and with everyone in the synagogue watching, He said, "Today this Scripture is fulfilled in your hearing" (Luke 4:21).

Jesus was basically telling the people that this Scripture was speaking of Him and that He was anointed by God. If the people believed His message that He was anointed, then they could release their faith to receive from God. If they chose not to believe that He was anointed, then there was no connection made with the anointing that was upon Him, therefore they would not receive.

## ONLY THOSE WHO BELIEVED

Many Christians think that all the sick people around Jesus were healed by Him. But that's unscriptural. Many people in the crowds were only curiosity seekers. Others were skeptics and mockers. Those without faith did not receive. Those who believed He was anointed would come into contact with that anointing by their faith and receive what they needed.

In my own ministry, I tell people that the Lord has placed a divine healing gift upon my life. I share that in my meetings because in a visitation I had one time from the Lord He personally told me to tell the people about this miracle healing anointing that He has given to me. If they don't believe, then they hinder themselves from receiving through my ministry.

Sharing that the Lord has anointed me builds faith in the people to receive from God. This is not the only anointing I have from the Lord, but it certainly is a primary one that operates in my ministry.

Be faithful to operate in the anointing that you currently have. Through faithfulness and diligence, God can see fit to place a new mantle of increased anointing upon you.

CHAPTER 3

# *The Biblical Pattern*

The classic Bible example of receiving a mantle is the Old Testament story of Elijah, the prophet, and Elisha, his servant.

In the Book of Second Kings chapter 2, we read about how Elijah's earthly ministry was drawing to a close. By the power of the Holy Spirit, the old prophet had accomplished much for God. Elijah would soon be going home in dramatic fashion, but there was still some more business he had to wrap up before leaving. Elijah decided to make one more round to visit the prophetic schools that he had overseen. Three towns were visited, and each town that they went to was a decrease in elevation.

*Then Elijah said to Elisha, "Stay here, please, for the Lord has sent me on to Bethel." But Elisha said, "As the Lord lives, and as your soul lives, I will not leave you!" So they went down to Bethel* (2 Kings 2:2).

They traveled from Gilgal down to Bethel, and then further down to Jericho. When you walk uprightly with the Lord, it sometimes seems like you are going backward or down instead of up. Often when you are at your lowest point is when you are closest to receiving your miracle.

Elisha, Elijah's servant, was determined to go with him, but before going to visit each town in which the schools were located, the old prophet tried to discourage the younger servant from coming along. Many people have often wondered why Elijah would do this to his only potential successor of the ministry. Often times, God will intentionally allow the journey toward destiny to be difficult and filled with many opportunities to quit, just to see if a person really wants it as much as he or she says.

Elisha needed to realize that nothing from Heaven comes cheap. The anointing of God must be highly valued and greatly appreciated by the one who receives it. After three gut-wrenching opportunities to stay behind and miss his miracle, Elisha persevered and was rewarded with the most important question he had ever been asked:

*Now Elijah took his **mantle**, rolled it up, and struck the water; and it was divided this way and that, so that the two of them crossed over on dry ground. And so it was, when they had crossed over, that Elijah said to Elisha, "**Ask! What may I do for you, before I am taken away from you?**"* (2 Kings 2:8-9)

Before Elisha was ever presented with this question, I believe he already knew it was coming. After all, he was prophetically inclined due to the calling of God upon his life and his close association with Elijah. Throughout the day, I am sure he pondered upon what his answer would be. Notice that when he was asked, he did not reply by saying, "I'm not sure, can I get back to you on that?" There was no hesitation in his response. After just seeing the miracle working power of God demonstrated only moments earlier through the parting of the Jordan River and then crossing over on dry ground, Elisha was now more settled in his heart than ever before as to what his answer would be. He knew exactly what he wanted and proceeded to ask in confident faith, expecting his request to be granted.

> *...Elisha said, "Please let a **double portion** of your spirit be upon me." So he said, "You have asked a hard thing, Nevertheless, if you see me when I am taken from you, it shall be so for you; but if not, it shall not be so"* (2 Kings 2:9-10).

See, when you get around the anointing of God, you change from the inside out. Jesus becomes your greatest desire and all that the world has to offer fades dimly away. Constantly being in an atmosphere where the glory of God was experienced made it easy for Elisha to ask for that which was most important to fulfill God's plan for his life.

Notice Elijah responded by saying, "You have asked a hard thing." He did not mean it would be hard for God to give him a double portion. Nothing is too difficult with God. He was simply trying to convey that this type of ministry is very tough and not for the faint at heart. A double portion would certainly attract much more ridicule and persecution than what would normally be expected for a prophet to endure. Elijah was revealing to Elisha the flip side of ministry that the public does not see. The loneliness, being misunderstood, not fitting in with others who live a compromised lifestyle, a high level of personal consecration, and being a top target for the powers of darkness were all challenges certain to face Elisha at every turn. In the eyes of Elijah, I am sure there was that not-so-hasty look of caution that expressed the thought of, "Are you sure this is what you want?" However, Elisha's mind was made up. He had already settled the issue in his heart and was ready to accept the destiny that awaited him.

By this point the deal was as good as done. As they continued their walk, they carried on a close conversation just as a father and son would do who genuinely love each other. We know the relationship they shared was very deep, for when Elisha saw Elijah taken up into Heaven, the first words out of his mouth were, "My father, my father." As they went, suddenly there appeared a chariot of fire pulled by horses of fire that swooped down and picked Elijah up, separating Elijah from Elisha. The horse-drawn fiery chariot carried Elijah up in a circular motion into Heaven as Elisha looked on in awe. With this sovereign act of God, one generation has now passed off the scene and the next generation now stands prepared to carry on the work of God.

*Then it happened, as they continued on and talked, that suddenly a chariot of fire appeared with horses of fire, and separated the two of them; and Elijah went up by a whirlwind into* *heaven. And Elisha saw it, and he cried out, "My father, my father, the chariot of Israel and its horsemen!" So he saw him no more. And he took hold of his own clothes and tore them into two pieces. He also took up the **mantle of Elijah** that had fallen from him, and went back and stood by the bank of the Jordan. Then he took the mantle of Elijah that had fallen from him, and struck the water, and said, "Where is the Lord God of Elijah?" And when he also had struck the water, it was divided this way and that; and Elisha crossed over* (2 Kings 2:11-14).

Notice that Elisha did not say, "Where is Elijah?" He said, "Where is the *Lord* God of Elijah?" In my heart today I believe many saints in the Body of Christ will soon be asking this very same question. The Church is presently at a stage where a great transition is taking place. Some of the greatest and most respected ministers in the Body of Christ today are in their eighties and nineties, having lived a long and blessed life. They will soon be going home to receive their reward in Heaven, but what are we to do when they leave? Thank God we have the answer. We are to do exactly what Elisha did and walk forward into a deeper level of the anointing of God.

## THEIR CEILING SHOULD BE OUR FLOOR

Some of these leading ministers have been in the ministry for over fifty years. Because they laid their lives down for the sake of the Gospel we can now reap the rewards of their knowledge and experience. In actuality, their ceiling should be the floor that we step over onto. Their many years of wisdom and experience can be downloaded into our spirits through diligent study and prayer so that we can complete the assignment of preaching the Gospel to the whole world.

When Elijah was taken up to Heaven, he was in the middle of a conversation with Elisha. Notice that Elijah was not off somewhere in private prayer just waiting to get whisked off the planet. No, he was busy pouring all he could into his successor. We'll have time to rest when we get to the other side. But as for now we have plenty of work to do. Some of the great preachers such as John Wesley preached right up until the day they died. The more one knows, then the more that one is responsible for passing it on to others. The older generation has a responsibility to impart their wisdom and knowledge into the hearts of those who will some day take their place.

So we have seen the obvious transference of the anointing that was upon Elijah's life now being placed upon Elisha! In the Bible, there are eight recorded miracles that Elijah performed. Did Elisha receive the full double portion that he asked for? If you count the miracles that are recorded in Elisha's ministry, you will see that he did 15 in his lifetime, just one short of the double portion. Someone may say, "See there, God didn't keep His word." But hold on a minute, that's not the end of the story. Something very interesting happened *after* Elisha died.

*Then Elisha died and was buried. Groups of Moabite raiders used to invade the land each spring. Once when some Israelites were burying a man, they spied a band of these raiders. So they hastily threw the corpse into the tomb of Elisha and fled. But as soon as the body touched Elisha's bones, the dead man revived and jumped to his feet! (2 Kings 13:20-21 NLT)*

With the miracle of Elisha's bones raising the dead man back to life, you can now bring the total up to 16! There it is, the double portion.

Honestly, we need a double portion compared to what those before us walked in. There needs to be a greater increase in firepower to offset the rise of darkness in the earth. Sin is increasing but so is the glory of God. Don't just desire the mantle, desire a double portion to offset the inflation of sin. So, we see from the Bible that mantles can be transferred from one individual to another.

I believe it is the Lord's will for mantles to be transferred to the generation that succeeds the former generation. Mantles should not fall and remain dormant but should be handed off and put into use by the fresh troops arriving on the scene. There is a group that should be looking to pass the relay baton and there is a group that should be looking to receive the handoff. A dear pastor couple that are precious friends of mine in Albuquerque, New Mexico, experienced a classic example of how the baton should be passed. The wife is the preaching-teaching pastor and her husband is the co-pastor and worship leader of this church. They make a great couple together in ministry. They spoke to me of how they heard of a very anointed minister who was in his eighties with a ministry marked by solid preaching and powerful miracles of healing. This minister had acquired and used the enormous tent that healing evangelist Jack Coe once used for his ministry.

This dear man had traveled throughout America preaching the Word and seeing the power of the Holy Spirit displayed in tent meetings. The pastor couple in Albuquerque felt led of the Spirit to contact this man and invite him to minister at their church. Upon contacting him, they asked him when he would like to come, and to their surprise he said, "I feel I need to come as soon as possible." The pastor couple thought that meant in several months, but he said, "No, I need to come *real soon*," and so they arranged for him to be at their church at the earliest possible time which was in two weeks.

Once he arrived, they immediately felt a divine connection in the Spirit. The meetings were outstanding as the minister moved in the gifts of the Spirit and demonstrated God's power through the strong anointing that God had bestowed upon his life. The pastor of this church told me that throughout the meetings this old minister seemed to be having such a wonderful time ministering. He laughed often and was clearly having fun as he taught the Word to the people. He got so happy in the Spirit he even ran around the sanctuary a few times in the middle of his preaching! Upon the minister's request the pastor even drove him through a certain area of Albuquerque where decades before, this man had once held a tent revival meeting. The pastor could tell that this older minister enjoyed recalling the memories of those former meetings as he pointed out where the main tent once stood, where the healing tent was, and where the accompanying children's tent was located. These were precious memories that reminded him of his many years of labor in God's vineyard as he looked forward to receiving his inheritance that was laid up in store for him in Heaven.

Just before the meetings ended, the minister did something the pastor and her husband did not expect. He laid his hands on the pastor couple and the assistant pastor and released his mantle to fully rest upon them. He held nothing back; he openly and publicly imparted to them every grace and mantle that he carried. It was a glorious moment, one of those divine appointments that only God can plan and cause to take place. After the meetings concluded, the minister flew home. Seven days later the pastor called the minister to speak with him, and the person who answered the phone shared that the minister was no longer alive, that he died two days ago!

## PASSING THE MANTLE

I used to run track all through high school and college. I always liked watching the sprint relays because they were very exciting. In relay races you have an "exchange zone" in which you must make the baton pass. If you do not make the baton pass quick enough and run out of the zone, then the team is disqualified. Each handoff and each reception of the baton from runner to runner must take place within the *zone*. It blesses me to see how that older minister passed the mantle while he still had time. Too many ministers never released their mantles, nor did they raise up a successor to continue on in their stead before they died. We should all plan for the future and prepare to make things as easy as possible for those who will transition in after our job is done. As an old man, Jacob blessed his twelve sons and prophesied over each one of them. After he blessed them, he put his feet up in the bed and died. That's cutting it pretty close, but the baton still was passed within the zone. What I love about the Lord is that He is still not hindered even when there is human failure. The Lord can still cause mantles to be transferred even if there are gaps of hundreds of years in between! The zone of exchange for heavenly mantles is quite large in the realm of the spirit. All things are possible with God. Are you ready to receive the mantle the Lord has for you?

# CHAPTER 4

# *Mantles Throughout the Old Testament*

Throughout the Bible and church history, the transferring of mantles has been well documented. Let's look at a few examples from the Bible and then we will observe other examples displayed in the annals of church history.

## MOSES AND JOSHUA

*Now Joshua the son of Nun was full of the spirit of wisdom, for Moses had laid his hands on him; so the children of Israel heeded him, and did as the Lord had commanded Moses* (Deuteronomy 34:9).

*After the death of Moses the servant of the Lord, it came to pass that the Lord spoke to Joshua the son of Nun, Moses'* *assistant, saying: "No man shall be able to stand before you all the days of your life; **as I was with Moses, so I will be with you...**"* (Joshua 1:1,5).

It is apparent that Joshua closely followed Moses. Notice how Joshua 1:1 states that Joshua was the assistant of Moses. In order to receive a mantle you must find some way to make a connection with that person. Joshua made this connection with Moses through serving him. I'm sure Joshua ran many errands for Moses. No doubt some of the serving he did was mundane and behind the scenes of the public eye.

## START WITH A SERVANT'S HEART

It's hard to find good servants even today. Promotion always comes after faithful serving. Even in my own life I didn't just happen to end up with an international ministry that mysteriously fell into my lap. For years, I served another pastor, being faithful where the Lord had me. I know what it is to clean the church toilets and vacuum the carpet once everybody else has left. I would polish all the wooden pews in the church until not a fingerprint could be found on them. Once a week I would wash my pastor's car and wax it to a brilliant shine. All these things I did without being asked, I just wanted to serve and I had no thoughts of pulpit ministry. So many people today want to jump straight to the top, but they have never gone through the serving process. There's no other way to long term success without a servant's heart.

Through the long process of Joshua serving the man of God, something happened to Joshua. Being so close to Moses certainly allowed incredible leadership skills to rub off on him, but he also received a much greater transfer than great administrative gifting.

> *So the LORD spoke to Moses face to face, as a man speaks to his friend. And he would return to the camp, **but his servant Joshua the son of Nun, a young man, did not depart from the tabernacle*** (Exodus 33:11).

Moses had taken his tent and placed it far outside the camp. He called it the Tent of Meeting. Anyone who wanted to consult with the Lord would go there. As Moses would go into the tent, all the Israelites would watch him go until he disappeared inside. It was inside of this tent that the Lord would speak to Moses face to face because of their friendship. All the people would see the glory cloud come down and hover at the entrance while the Lord spoke to Moses. What's amazing to me is that after Moses would leave the tent, we see that Joshua continued to stay inside the tent. The glory of God is returning to our churches in America and as it increases we are going to see the young people not want to leave! There will be a sudden loss of interest in video games and other worldly forms of entertainment. When the glory of God begins to show up, the young people won't care what's on television or what's playing at the movie theaters.

These times of refreshing have been pre-set by the Lord for the equipping of His great end-time army. After the equipping will come the "sending out" to this nation and to the four corners of the earth. When God's Spirit moves in power it won't be necessary to get a six-year degree from a seminary. A few months in the glory will impart a "knowing" of what to do. Yes, we will still need proper Bible training and equipping centers, but courses will be accelerated and understanding will come quickly. The old fashioned Pentecostals had a good way of describing it. They would say, "It's better caught than taught." I agree with that statement. The new style of Bible training will not only emphasize biblical teaching, but will understand the importance of impartation. The students will *catch it* and run with the message.

## ELIJAH, ELISHA, BUT NOT GEHAZI

In the first chapter, we examined the mantle that was passed on from the prophet Elijah to his servant Elisha. It is my belief, based upon careful study of the Scriptures, that Elisha's servant Gehazi had a place reserved for him in the prophetic ministry. Elisha received the mantle from Elijah because of his proven growth and maturity in the ways of God. Elisha was well trained and qualified to receive the mantle of Elijah.

However, Gehazi missed a once in a lifetime opportunity because of his love of money. Keep in mind that there is nothing wrong with money. It is the love of money that the Word of God tells us is the root of all evil. In the Book of Second Kings, chapter 5, we are given the account of how the Aramean army commander Naaman was healed of leprosy through the ministry of Elisha. Naaman was so thankful for his healing that he wanted to give a financial blessing to Elisha, but Elisha refused to receive it because it was not the right thing to do in this particular case. This was because Naaman's superior officer had originally contacted the King of Israel to request help for Naaman. The King of Israel was filled with fear when he received the letter, because he misunderstood the letter as not being sincere and he thought the Arameans were trying to somehow start a war (see Kings 5:1-7). It was at this time that Elisha was informed of the situation so he stepped in quickly and took charge before things got out of hand.

> *So it was, when Elisha the man of God, heard that the king of Israel had torn his clothes, that he sent to the king saying, "Why have you torn your clothes? Please let him come to me, and he shall know that there is a prophet in Israel"* (2 Kings 5:8).

Knowing the full story helps us better understand why Elisha never took the offering that Naaman presented. If there was an offering to be given, it would only be proper for it to be presented to the king of Israel because it was in the king's hands that the original request had been placed. Elisha did, however, receive two mules loaded with supplies from Naaman as compensation for his time, but he did not touch the king's reward which was offered to him, which was ten talents of silver, six thousand pieces of gold, and ten changes of fine clothing. By doing this, Elisha passed one of the most important tests that a person could ever face—the money test. Unfortunately, Elisha's servant Gehazi did not fare so well under this same temptation.

> *Gehazi, the servant of Elisha the man of God, said to himself, "My master was too easy on Naaman, this Aramean, by not accepting from him what he brought. As surely as the Lord lives,* **I will run after him and get something from**

*him. So Gehazi hurried after Naaman. When Naaman saw him running toward him, he got down from the chariot to meet him. "Is everything all right?" he asked. "Everything is all right," Gehazi answered.*

*"My master sent me to say, "Two young men from the company of the prophets have just come to me from the hill country of Ephraim. Please give them a talent of silver and two sets of clothing." "By all means, take two talents," said Naaman. He urged Gehazi to accept them, and then tied up the two talents of silver in two bags, with two sets of clothing. He gave them to two of his servants, and they carried them ahead of Gehazi. When Gehazi came to the hill, he took the things from the servants and put them away in the house. He sent the men away and they left. Then he went in and stood before his master Elisha.*

*"Where have you been, Gehazi?" Elisha asked.*

*"Your servant didn't go anywhere," Gehazi answered.*

*But Elisha said to him, "Was not my spirit with you when the man got down from his chariot to meet you? Is this the time to take money, or accept clothes, olive groves, vineyards, flocks, herds, or menservants, and maidservants? Naaman's leprosy will cling to you and to your descendants forever." Then Gehazi went from Elisha's presence and he was leprous, as white as snow* (2 Kings 5:20-27 NIV).

It's interesting to see that Gehazi said, "I will run after him, and get something from him." Whenever a person runs after money he or she is in for trouble. Gehazi should have run after God, faithfully served Elisha, and in due time the blessing of the

Lord would have come. Gehazi failed to understand that the anointing of the Holy Spirit actually attracts wealth. Today, God still wants His people to prosper financially, but it must come in His timing. Often there are many tests that the Lord will allow His children to go through before He takes them into their wealthy place, but by walking in the love of God and exercising faith and patience, all the promises of God can be obtained.

Let's not overlook the *rest of the story* concerning how some time down the road the Lord eventually blessed Elisha with financial abundance.

> *Elisha went to Damascus, the capital of Aram, where King Ben-hadad lay sick. When someone told the king that the man of God had come, the king said to Hazael, "Take a gift to the man of God. Then tell him to ask the Lord 'Will I recover from this illness?'"* **So Hazael loaded down forty camels with the finest products of Damascus as a gift for Elisha.** *He went to him and said, "Your servant Ben-hadad, the king of Aram, has sent me to ask, 'Will I recover from this illness?'"* (2 Kings 8:7-9 NLT).

God blessed Elisha with forty camels loaded with the finest products of Damascus. A camel's long, thin legs have powerful muscles which allow the animal to carry heavy loads over long distances. A camel can carry as much as 990 pounds, but a normal and more comfortable cargo weight is 330 pounds. The weight they were carrying is not exactly known, but it's obvious there were a lot of valuable items taken to Elisha because of the large caravan of camels sent, and the fact that the Scripture tells us the camels were burdened, or fully loaded. The term describing the present that was given as the *finest products* can also be translated as *the rarest and most exquisite of the land.*

Too bad Gehazi was not around when the camels showed up. He would have gotten a whole lot more than two suits and a few hundred dollars that he sold out for. The covenant we have with God through the shed blood of Jesus includes financial provision. We should not make this the primary focus of our lives because it is just one facet of the many blessings of God. But we should not ignore it or apologize for it either.

> *The blessing of the Lord brings wealth, and he adds no trouble to it* (Proverbs 10:22 NIV).

That leaves us with the question of what happened to the original mantle of Elijah? Elijah passed his mantle to Elisha but we do not find it openly revealed in Scripture who it was that received the mantle of Elisha.

One thing I have discovered in my walk with the Lord is that nothing from Heaven comes cheap. The gifts of God are priceless and if there is not a qualified candidate to receive them, then the gifts will be kept in holding until the right person is available.

## ELIJAH'S MANTLE—WHERE IS IT?

What happened to Elijah's mantle? Fortunately, we have a reliable and well-preserved Jewish tradition that sheds light onto this mystery. Jewish tradition teaches that after Elisha died, there was not a suitable individual to receive Elijah's mantle.

**Upon the death of Elisha, the mantle was taken and placed in the holy place of the tabernacle just to the right of the altar of incense.** There it was kept until the prophet Jeremiah removed it from Jerusalem and took it into hiding to protect it from the invading Babylonian armies of Nebuchadnezzar.

From the time of Jeremiah we skip hundreds of years forward to the time of Zacharias and Elizabeth. The first chapter of Luke's Gospel tells us that both Zacharias and Elizabeth were old, and that they had no child because Elizabeth was barren. It's amazing to notice how the majority of the great women of the Bible were barren. Elizabeth, Sarah, Rachel, Leah, Elkanah, Hannah, and the mother of Samson were all unable to conceive seed. Yet, God did a miracle in each of their lives and they all became pregnant and gave birth.

Zacharias was of the priestly order of Abijah and was chosen by lot during his week of service to burn incense when he went into the temple. As he was in the temple carrying out his duties, a supernatural encounter took place.

> *Then an angel of the Lord appeared to him,* **standing on the right side of the altar of incense** (Luke 1:11).

Notice the position of where the angel appeared to Zacharias. It was at the right of the altar of incense where Elijah's mantle was believed to have been stored. Many Jewish scholars believe that as John the Baptist grew into a young man and headed into the desert to prepare for his ministry of being a forerunner for the Lord, that his father took the original mantle of Elijah from the temple and gave it to John. One thing is for sure, John the Baptist walked in the spirit and power of Elijah. The Lord will find, call, and develop those whom He desires to mantle with heavenly authority.

## ELIJAH AND JOHN THE BAPTIST

Concerning John the Baptist, the Holy Spirit foretold through the prophet Malachi saying:

> *Behold, I will send you Elijah the prophet before the coming of the great and dreadful day of the Lord* (Malachi 4:5).

Jesus also spoke of John during his earthly ministry:

> *The disciples asked him, "Why then do the teachers of the law say that Elijah must come first?" Jesus replied, "To be sure, Elijah comes and will restore all things. But I tell you,* **Elijah has already come, and they did not recognize him,** *but have done to him everything they wished. In the same way the Son of Man is going to suffer at their hands."* **Then the disciples understood that he was talking to them about John the Baptist** (Matthew 17:10-13 NIV).

## CONNECTING IN THE SPIRIT

Mantles are very interesting because they allow you to connect in the Spirit with perhaps someone you have never met or seen in person. John the Baptist could not have met Elijah because Elijah lived hundreds of years earlier. Yet John received the mantle of Elijah. It is important to understand that there is no distance in the spirit realm. The presence of the Holy Spirit upon one's life demonstrated through the symbolic representation of a mantle allows a person to identify with the one who originally wore the mantle. The identification can sometimes be so strong that it will even influence the way a person may dress. For instance, have you ever wondered why John the Baptist wore the same kind of clothing that Elijah did? The following two verses speak about this.

*Then he said to them, "What kind of man was it who came up to meet you and told you these words?" So they answered him, "A hairy man wearing a leather belt around his waist." And he said, "It is Elijah the Tishbite"* (2 Kings 1:7-8).

*For this is he who was spoken of by the prophet Isaiah, saying;*
*"The voice of one crying in the wilderness:*
*'Prepare the way of the Lord;*
*Make His paths straight.'"*
*Now John himself was clothed in camel's hair, with a leather belt around his waist; and his food was locusts and wild honey* (Matthew 3:3-4).

Did you notice how Elijah and John both had the same style of clothing? That is because it is the same Holy Spirit that was upon each of them. The same Spirit that anointed Elijah as a mighty prophet also anointed John the Baptist to be a prophet and a forerunner of the coming of the Lord Jesus Christ. Although the personality that God gave you is unique, it is possible for a mantle to influence certain areas of your life in a similar way that it influenced the previous person.

Both Elijah and John wore rough clothing. I don't know how they did it without wearing a tee shirt underneath. The itching and rubbing of coarse camel hair would drive me crazy. I couldn't preach in camel clothes because I'd be too busy scratching my back and chest! I guess after a while a person would get used to it, but I'd hate to go through the transition process. But that is what their calling required, and to them it was most likely enjoyable and invigorating.

The similarities that can occur between two individuals when a mantle is passed on can be quite amazing. In my own life when I received the first mantle that the Lord had for me, which was worn by a former prophet, I was very surprised to find out some unique and similar traits we both shared. Through research I found an old book that had been written about this man's life. As I read through the pages I was surprised to see similarities that we both had, even though we lived many years apart.

I have found regarding mantles that the anointing you wish to receive from the Lord cannot always be seen upon one particular person. That is why there can be multiple mantles placed upon your life. I think the story of Joseph with his long coat of many colors is a shadowing of this truth.

> *Now Israel loved Joseph more than all his children, because he was the son of his old age. Also he made him a tunic of many colors* (Genesis 37:3).

Those many colors that Joseph wore represent various types of the anointing that are available for you to receive from the Lord. I have received mantles from individuals whose particular anointing pertained to a deeper spiritual walk with the Lord. But I also feel a connection with those ministers who have gone before us that demonstrated other areas of excellence in their lives, such as living in divine health and having a strong apostolic authority in the realm of finances. There should be a balance in our lives where we excel in our spiritual development while at the same time demonstrating good common sense in life.

I've always admired the life of Charles Harrison Mason who was the founder of the Church of God in Christ, which is the largest African-American Pentecostal denomination in the world. When I was a young man in my early twenties, the Holy Spirit led me to attend a local Church of God in Christ while I was living in Lubbock, Texas. That particular church had a membership of around 200 people and I was the only member who was not an African-American. However, the church family greatly loved me and I especially enjoyed singing in the choir on Sunday mornings. If you've ever wondered where I learned to shout and holler the way I do when I preach, then there's your answer. It was in that church. At that time we didn't think it was a very good service unless the preacher got to shoutin' and hollerin' and we all would be so physically expended after the service that we needed six days to recover!

I was there for a little over two years and it was in that church where the Lord began to raise me up in the ministry. I was appointed the Men's Assistant Sunday School Teacher for the Sunday morning sessions. The only problem was that the main teacher would hardly ever show up to teach! He would maybe teach once a month, but the other times he would simply never show up, which by default made me the teacher. It was difficult teaching men who were often two or three times my age, but it forced me to get into the Word and study so I would be prepared and not be caught off guard. My pastor at that time would often share stories with me about Charles Harrison Mason who was truly an apostle to the body of Christ. One of the main things I like so much about Brother Mason is that he lived to be 95 years of age. That's rare for someone to do who carries an international ministry. Most ministers who have a large ministry such as his often wear out and leave life early, many just barely crossing over the age of seventy. Just think of the difference an extra ten or twenty years could make in regard to storing up eternal rewards for the other side of glory. You know for sure I'm claiming a portion of that mantle. Glory to God! I desire long life that I might be able to do more for the Lord.

## A MANTLE FOR FINANCES

It's important to also have a mantle for finances, especially in the last days that we are living in. Some people try to act super-spiritual and pretend like finances are not important, but one of the most important things you can do as a Christian to promote a good testimony is to pay your bills on time. Multiple mantles are available for you to walk in just as Joseph had that beautiful long tunic that had all of those wonderful colors. There is a mantle for finances that God has for you! This is an area that you have to be careful in. I would encourage you not to follow someone's ministry who uses guilt manipulation to obtain money, is an outright beggar, or is known to be irresponsible in financial matters. Rather, I would encourage you to seek a genuine financial anointing from the Lord and emulate those who excel in finances and who also demonstrate high integrity and strong character. Joseph was just such a person. Even today, the Lord is preparing certain saints to walk in end-time financial stewardship that they may have an abundance to support the Lord's Kingdom plans in the earth. There will be many "Josephs" that the Lord will entrust with wealth. It requires special preparation, but as you are faithful with what He has given you, eventually a financial mantle can fall upon your shoulders.

I have found that qualifying for a financial mantle can be one of the toughest mantles to receive. When I say "qualify" I don't mean in the sense of earning it through your own good works. On the cross, Jesus became poor that we, through His poverty, might be rich; so the divine exchange has already taken place. However, this is an inheritance we must obtain by faith, and you'll find that the devil will put up a pretty good fight in trying to keep you back when it comes to finances. That's because the enemy of our souls has a lot of leverage when it comes to money because he is the god of this world.

> *But even if our gospel is veiled, it is veiled to those who are perishing,* **whose minds the god of this age has blinded...** (2 Corinthians 4:3-4).

Satan is the god of this age and the prince of the power of the air. Satan doesn't mind one bit if a drug dealer drives a new luxury car, but he sure doesn't want a Christian to drive one. He tries to blind the minds of the unsaved and even Christians to think that it is holy to be poor. Satan takes great delight in sending forth his demons to support beer companies, cigarette makers, drug cartels, and other forms of vice and supports them through his demonic agents of darkness to generate tons of money. But the Bible says that the financial blessing of the Lord does not bring sorrow or trouble (see Proverbs 10:22). When the blessing comes from the Lord, then you can sleep at night in total peace because you haven't earned money in a way that gives you a guilty conscience.

The Lord could not give a lot of money to most of His people because it would destroy them. Money is a tool, a means of authority and can be easily misused. Many people with large amounts of money who do not have a close walk with the Lord use their money to manipulate and control others. Money is leverage and it can easily influence others. That's why if a person genuinely desires to be a vessel fit for the Master's use, then there must be proper training involving financial stewardship. Job in the Bible was a man whom God could trust with great wealth. Yet even Job went through times of testing, but in the end, God brought him out with twice as much as he had before.

About a year ago my wife and I went over to visit some good friends of ours who were going through a very difficult time financially. The husband had previously been earning a very good net income of over $350,000 a month. But his business suffered a major setback that was completely unexpected and eventually the whole thing shut down. On top of his business failure he was served legal papers stating that he was being sued for a large amount of money. This whole series of events sent my friend into a mental depression that lasted over a year.

He had fallen from such a high place and was now struggling to pay his basic utility bills while also having fallen behind on his rent. He had gone from living in a massive luxury home to a little tiny cabin back in the woods with his family.

When I talked with him, he reminded me of Job who was so perplexed that he was perplexed with his perplexities! However, as we shared dinner together in their little cabin and talked about the Lord, we began to laugh as we realized that God was doing a deep work in this man's life. As we sat at the table, I happened to look over to the side and to my surprise I saw Job himself sitting in a chair in the corner of the room! But he wasn't the Job who was sad, depressed, and ruined. It was the Job who had come out on the other side and had developed a deeper walk with God through his trials and difficulties. In this vision I actually saw Job sitting there, and I'll tell you one thing, he was looking mighty good. He looked middle-eastern with deep, dark, sparkling eyes and he had on a beautiful robe. He had a long flowing white beard that reached all the way to his chest. He looked magnificent! I turned to my friend at the table and said, "Cheer up, you are coming out of this and your fiery trial has ended. God will now raise you back up just as he did Job." It was only a few months after this that God began to lift this man back up in financial strength. He was offered and accepted a position as Vice President of Sales for a major international health related corporation. The money is flowing strong again, and needless to say, he is no longer living in that tiny, cramped little cabin. Even the legal troubles he was facing are being resolved in a peaceful way. The best part of all is that he views his purpose of having prosperity as being a means not just for himself, but to be led by the Holy Spirit in ways that he might further the Lord's Kingdom in the earth.

## STANDING IN FAITH FOR GOD'S BEST

This is another reason you should be careful with whom you align yourself. I've read many stories where saints of God have taken vows of poverty because they considered wealth and riches to be evil. In reality, what they were doing was joining themselves to a curse. There is nothing holy about poverty. It is a product of the curse that came upon the world through Adam's sin. But we have dominion over lack and poverty through our faith in the Lord Jesus Christ. In my heart, I believe the reason some of the great saints of previous generations took vows of poverty was because they desired a walk with God where they would not be distracted with worldly cares. I believe their motives were certainly right, but they went about it the wrong way. Money is not evil. It is neutral and can be used for good or evil depending upon who has it. I believe the Lord today is looking for those who are willing to make "vows of prosperity." Along with a "vow of prosperity" it would be good to make a "vow of humility" to keep one's feet firmly planted on solid ground. We should be willing to stand in faith for God's very best. We should embrace the full covenant blessings that Jesus purchased for us at Calvary. Let the Holy Spirit lead you regarding the financial mantle He has for you.

Be open to the multiple and various mantles that you need to walk in victory in every area of your life. While visiting with a dear minister friend recently, who is much older then myself, he shared with me that he counted up all the mantles he knew of that he had received in his life. When I asked him how many he could identify, he said, "I've counted twenty-seven of them." I encourage you to step into that multicolored tunic similar to what Joseph wore and be clothed with the full provision that God has for you.

# CHAPTER 5

# *A New Testament View of Mantles*

Although you will not find the word *mantle* in the New Testament Scriptures, the principle still applies today. Keep in mind that before Jesus went to the cross, much of the emphasis throughout the Old Testament was placed upon *exterior* or *outward* things. For example, under the Old Covenant, all of the male Israelites were required to be circumcised, as God instructed Abraham in the following verses.

> *This is my covenant with you and your descendants after you, the covenant you are to keep: Every male among you shall be circumcised. You are to undergo circumcision, and it will be the sign of the covenant between Me and you* (Genesis 17:10-11 NIV).

This physical act of circumcision was an *outward* act that joined God's people in a covenant relationship with Him. Today, as a New Testament Christian, you *do not* have to be physically circumcised to be in a right relationship with God. We see this clearly outlined for us in the New Testament, such as in the following verse:

> *When you came to Christ, you were "circumcised," but not by a physical procedure. Christ performed a circumcision—the cutting away of your sinful nature* (Colossians 2:11 NLT).

When we receive Jesus Christ as our personal Lord and Savior, the old sinful nature is "cut-off," or circumcised by God, and we receive new life within our spirit. Through this example, can you see how God desires to place the emphasis on the *inward* heart of man, rather than the *outward* physical man? The same transition from the Old Covenant to the New Covenant regarding foods has also taken place. This is an area where many New Testament Christians continually try to get back under the Mosaic Law.

I know Christians who would be shocked if they saw me eat a shrimp or a porkchop. In order not to offend them, I wouldn't eat it in front of them because their understanding of these things is limited and it would offend their conscience. The Old Testament food groups that were classified as "unclean" were foods that were represented as types and shadows. God was endeavoring to speak symbolically to His people through these foods. The whole point God was trying to make was the importance of keeping yourself pure and clean to avoid sin. The unclean foods represented sin. (See Leviticus 11 and Deuteronomy 14:3-21.)

Under the New Covenant, you can eat pork if you want to. To me, it doesn't taste that good, so I rarely eat it, but that's a personal matter of taste and preference. Some teach that the "unclean" foods are unhealthy for you. While I would prefer to eat higher on the food chain, such as a piece of halibut over a piece of catfish, I am still free in Christ to eat catfish if I want to. A few years ago the oldest man in the world died. He lived in China and was 127 years old when he passed away, and was often featured in leading newspapers around the world. In one interview just before he died, he was asked his secret of longevity. His confident response was, "White rice and good pork!" This man ate white rice, which has hardly any nutritional value, and pork, which is very fattening, and eventually died as the world's oldest man, verified by his authentic birth certificate. Consider the following Scriptures **from the New Testament** regarding food:

> *They forbid people to marry and **order them to abstain from certain foods**, which God created to be received with thanksgiving by those who believe and who know the truth. **For <u>everything</u> God created is good, and <u>nothing</u> is to be rejected if it is received with thanksgiving,** because it is consecrated by the word of God and prayer* (1 Timothy 4:3-5 NIV).

This was written by Paul the apostle and he was as Jewish as a person can be, yet he understood the truth about food. Stop and think about it for a moment. How can eating a piece of fresh, grilled Blue Marlin (a fish without scales) make you unclean? How can a piece of fish make you unclean in the eyes of God? Isn't the blood of Jesus more powerful than a piece of fish? It's the blood of Jesus and His grace that justifies you before God, not your eating habits. The following verses by Paul should settle the argument forever regarding food. Please remember that these verses are from the New Covenant where we are saved by grace through faith, and not by our keeping a system of rules and regulations that only serve to magnify a person's shortcomings.

> *I know and am convinced by the Lord Jesus that there is* **nothing unclean of itself;** *but to him who considers anything to be unclean, to him it is unclean. Yet if your brother is grieved because of your food, you are no longer walking in love. Do not destroy with your food the one for whom Christ died* (Romans 14:14-15).

> *Don't tear apart the work of God over what you eat.* **Remember, all foods are acceptable,** *but it is wrong to eat something if it makes another person stumble* (Romans 14:20 NLT).

The fourteenth chapter of Romans is my favorite chapter in the Bible. Paul received personal revelation from the Lord that there is no food that is unclean. We know Paul is speaking about food because he references his statement of *nothing unclean to food* (see Rom. 14:14). You can eat non-kosher food because God gave the "green light" on all food as being edible. Of course, some foods are definitely healthier than others. It's a big world that we live in. Some cultures enjoy eating snakes, spiders, and bugs. Personally, I try to eat healthy and exercise often. There is some value to the dietary laws found in the Book of Leviticus as far as certain foods being more sanitary and healthy than others (see Lev. 11). We should all acquire a good understanding of how to eat healthy so that we are able to take good care of our bodies.

But again, the bigger picture is that of walking in love. As I said before, there are those who do not know about New Testament teaching along this line. If I ate a shrimp in front of them it would upset them. So, because I love them, I will keep my faith to myself and be careful never to put a stumbling block in front of them. This not only concerns food and drink but anything that would be a hindrance. The focus under the New Covenant is to be filled with the Holy Spirit and walk in love. The inward focus will produce the correct outward results.

In much the same way, the mantles spoken of in the Old Testament were only an *outward* representation of a specific anointing in which the Holy Spirit would manifest Himself upon a person. As I mentioned earlier, the mantle which Elijah the prophet wore had no supernatural power in and of itself. Under the Old Covenant, the mantle was only an outward representation of what was really a degree of anointing given by the Holy Spirit. There are many examples throughout the Old Testament of how God would anoint certain physical things to be used as an outward demonstration of God's power and glory. We see this in the story concerning the bones of the prophet Elisha.

*Then Elisha died and was buried. Groups of Moabite raiders used to invade the land each spring. Once, when some Israelites were burying a man, they spied a band of these raiders. So they hastily threw the corpse into the tomb of Elisha and fled. But as soon as the body touched Elisha's bones, the dead man revived and jumped to his feet!* (2 Kings 13:20-21 NLT)

What caused the dead man to come back to life when he touched the bones of Elisha? Were the bones of Elisha any different physically from the bones that you and I have? No, his bones were just like ours. The dead man was brought back to life because of the residual anointing of the Holy Spirit within the bones of Elisha. You could say that while he was alive he was *saturated* with the power and Presence of God.

In like fashion, if you go into a room that is full of people who are smoking cigarettes, you will come out smelling like cigarette smoke even if you do not smoke yourself. If you spend a lot of time with God in fellowship and prayer, then you will become saturated with His Holy Presence and He will get all over you. So it was not the bones (the outward evidence) that raised a man from the dead, but the anointing of the Holy Spirit. Follow along with me and grasp the truth that it is not a cloth or an animal skin (mantle) draped around someone's shoulders that enables him or her to do miracles. It is the Holy Spirit who works miracles through God's people!

We also see another example of this in the story found in the Old Testament Book of Judges concerning Samson and his long hair. Some Christians actually think that Samson's incredible, supernatural strength was because of his long hair. In my life I have met many guys with long hair, yet I never met one of them who could demonstrate the type of strength that Samson had. What was the source of Samson's great strength? Was it his long hair? Was it due to Samson having a Gold Card Membership at the local gym? Was it due to a high protein diet or an excessive consumption of red meat? No, it was none of those *outward* things. Then why was he so strong? He was strong because the Spirit of God was the source of his strength. When the Holy Spirit would come upon him, he would be transformed into a super-man. When he was under the anointing of the Spirit of God, it didn't matter if he was outnumbered a thousand to one. He was simply invincible as long as he stayed surrendered to the Lord.

An interesting story demonstrating Samson's great strength is found in the sixteenth chapter of the Book of Judges. Samson found himself trapped inside the city of Gaza with armed men set in ambush to take his life. Gaza was the primary stronghold of the Philistine nation and was well fortified with an enormous wall that encircled the city and it had two huge gates that were kept closed at night to protect the city. Some biblical scholars say the two gates of the city could have been as high as 65 feet and could have weighed as much as 100 tons! Yet Samson tore down the two massive gates with his bare hands. In doing so he also ripped the wooden posts and metal bars away that fastened the gates to the walls. Then, he put the two giant gates on his shoulders and carried them uphill almost 40 miles away toward the city of Hebron, which had an increased elevation of almost 3,000 feet, before putting them down near the top of a mountain. (See Judges 16:1-3.)

Believe me, there is no hairstyle in the world that will give you that kind of strength. This phenomenal act accomplished by Samson was actually the Holy Spirit moving upon him through the supernatural gift of the working of miracles. Oh, how we need to work in harmony with the Holy Spirit so that we might see the power of God manifested in our lives today!

## THE ANOINTING FOR SUPERNATURAL POWER

The same Holy Spirit that anointed Elisha's bones, which raised a man from the dead, also anointed Samson to be a real life super-man, and He can also anoint you with supernatural power. This is why the Holy Spirit who anointed a believer in times past can still anoint a child of God with the *same* anointing today. Mantles can be transferred because the Holy Spirit can transfer the anointing of God.

A close friend of mine who is a mature Spirit-filled believer shared with me how a seasoned prophet once gave him a prophetic word that the spirit of Samson would come upon him at times. My friend later did experience a Samson type of anointing when he was assisting in an exercise weight workout. My friend lives in Southern California and is 5′7″ tall and weighs around 155 pounds. He was spotting a very huge man who was performing leg squats with multiple repetitions of exactly 550 pounds. This man was an accomplished power-lifter and bodybuilder who was tall and weighed over 300 pounds with a highly developed muscular frame. My friend was there simply to give him a *spot*, which is when you give someone a slight amount of assistance on their lift to help them move through a possible sticking point.

The large power-lifter would squat the weights without a safety rack because he was confident of having no problem with the lift, having done this amount of weight many times before. He placed his huge shoulders beneath the bar to lift the massive weight off the rack. He then pushed out the first few reps as his gigantic legs strained under the heavy load. Suddenly, as he squatted down to do another rep he grimaced in pain as something in his back had just gotten pinched or strained. The unexpected pain caused him to lose his ability to lift the weight and now the weight was driving him downward without any support bars to break the fall.

Quickly my friend, without even thinking, reached down and grabbed the weight off of the man's shoulders and curled it up as if doing a biceps arm curl. He then extended the weight out and upward with his arms as he safely placed the weight back on the tall squat rack. The huge power-lifter looked up and said, "Did you just do what I think you did?" He answered, "Yes, I guess I did!" The same Holy Spirit who came upon Samson came upon my friend in a time of need right in the middle of the gym. This miracle strength has not been a one time event for him. He has actually had this type of anointing happen to him several times where he was able to lift a heavy weight in an emergency situation by the power of the Holy Spirit.

At another time he was asked by some friends to help and try to move a car that had gotten stuck in an ice hole. At this particular time my friend's back had been injured and he had trouble even moving because of the pain. However, at his friend's insistence he hobbled out of his car and endeavored to give what little help he could. He noticed that the stuck car had one tire completely sunk down into a hole. The car was actually resting on the bottom axle, which now lay on the ground because of the depth of the hole. As my friend reached down to grab the bumper and pull it upward, he fell over on the car with his hand still on the bumper because of the severe pain in his back. Now he wasn't pulling but was actually adding more weight because he was pushing down on the car with his own body weight. When that happened, the car was instantly lifted up out of the hole and pushed forward. The other men stepped back and said to my friend, "How did you do that?" He said, "Don't look at me, I wasn't even pulling. It was the power of God that moved the car." The same Holy Spirit who came upon Samson is in the earth today and His power is more than enough to see us through to victory.

## FIND YOUR PLACE OF ANOINTING

Basically, under the Old Covenant, a mantle was an outward representation of a specific anointing of the Holy Spirit. As a New Covenant child of God, you can be anointed by the Holy Spirit to accomplish the work that God has prepared for you to do. Find your place of anointing and do whatever it is with all your heart that God has called you to do.

So, even though we do not see the term "mantle" or "mantles" directly mentioned in the New Testament, we know that the Holy Spirit is actively involved in the Church today, in anointing God's people for service and ministry. I've always liked a well known verse in the Book of Hebrews that most Christians have memorized by heart.

*Jesus Christ is the same yesterday, today, and forever* (Hebrews 13:8).

This verse sends a clear message to New Testament believers that God is still a God who performs miracles today when His people reach out to Him in faith. God has never changed. Through His Church He still heals the sick and casts out demons. Miracles are for today. But there is also another clear implication of this verse, which when taken in context gives us a deeper appreciation for mantles. Hebrews 13:8 says;

*Remember your leaders, who spoke the word of God to you. Consider the outcome of their way of life and imitate their faith. Jesus Christ is the same yesterday and today and forever* (Hebrews 13:7-8 NIV).

Jesus Christ who anointed Paul is still the same Jesus today. Jesus Christ who anointed Charles Finney is still the same Jesus today. Jesus Christ who anointed John Wesley is still the same Jesus today and will continue to be so forever. God has not changed. He is still anointing His people and He will continue to. We are to remember our leaders in the Christian faith. Their mantles are available for the end-time church.

Paul and Timothy were two men who understood the concept of spiritual impartation and the importance of passing on a mantle.

## PAUL AND TIMOTHY

Paul and Timothy had a father and son type relationship. Writing to the Philippian Christians, Paul had this to say about Timothy:

*But you know his proven character, that as a son with his father he served with me in the gospel* (Philippians 2:22).

Here again we see a common way in which a mantle or anointing is transferred. Paul mentioned in the above Scripture that Timothy had served with him. Serving allows you to come into close association with a person, which in turn causes what is on that person to get over on you. One may reason that if Timothy had some of the anointing that was on Paul rub off on him, then why wasn't his ministry as well known as Paul's? The answer is that the ministry calling is different for each individual. God doesn't call every minister to have an international type ministry. For instance, not every pastor will have a large church with thousands of members. There are pastors whom God has called to shepherd a small flock of 100 members; yet they are still in the perfect will of God. Having a successful ministry is all relative to the specific assignment given to one by God.

Paul also speaks very highly of Timothy in the following statement:

*To Timothy, my dearly beloved son…* (2 Timothy 1:2 KJV).

For Paul to address Timothy so affectionately indicates to us the depth of their relationship. Only the Holy Spirit can form this kind of relationship. In your entire lifetime, you may have many friends, but you will only have a few spiritual fathers. It is not always the case, but often mantles are transferred from a spiritual father down to a spiritual son.

# CHAPTER 6

# *Examples Throughout Church History*

Now let's look at some more recent examples of mantles being transferred from one individual to another.

**Prophet Bob Jones**—The prophetic ministry of Bob Jones is known around the world. Bob Jones is esteemed as a prophet of the Lord and he also fits the Old Testament description of a Seer. Angelic visitations and heavenly experiences are regular occurrences for Bob. Examples of his visions such as, "The Baseball Game," and "The Bill of Rights," have blessed the lives of many people around the world. In 1987, Bob even spoke about a second space shuttle disaster (which occurred on February 1, 2003) and the spiritual implications that this event would entail. He has also accurately prophesied other major world events. Bob Jones' close friend and fellow minister of the Gospel, Paul Keith Davis of White Dove Ministries, describes in his January, 2003, ministry newsletter how Bob received the prophetic mantle he now walks in:

> Bob had three supernatural encounters as a young boy while living on a cotton farm in rural Arkansas. The first one occurred one August afternoon on a dusty road close to his home. As he was walking along this hot road, he saw something strange take place. He watched as a man riding on a white horse began galloping toward him from Heaven. Upon seeing this unusual sight, his mind could think of only one thing he heard often sung in the Baptist churches of Arkansas. He had always been taught that the angel Gabriel would someday appear and blow his trumpet signifying the end of the world. That was the first reaction he had upon seeing this supernatural being.
>
> The angelic messenger was carrying a unique silver trumpet that had one mouthpiece but two double horns which he blew. Even as a young boy, he knew this was the angel Gabriel. This identification has since been confirmed to him in subsequent experiences. Needless to say, he was quite terrified at the sight. Nothing was spoken at that time, but the messenger did carry, draped across the saddle, a mantle that looked very similar to the hide of an animal. It was something that appeared like a cowhide that Gabriel threw at Bob's feet. With that, the angel and horse vanished.

Bob has since discovered that this spiritual "mantle" was worn by a prophet from South Africa who formerly walked the rivers from village to village with a powerful ministry of truth and deliverance. Bob has also met the grandson of this man and discussed the ministry that he carried to his generation.[1]

**Dr. Peter Tan**—Dr. Tan's international teaching ministry demonstrates remarkable depth and revelation that has come forth out of a life devoted to prayer, fasting, and the study of God's Word. In 1994, Brother Tan was taken in the Spirit to Heaven and shown its glories and wonders. The amazing account of his visit entitled, "*Visitation to the Throne Room of God,*" is very uplifting and inspiring. The following is an account from Dr. Tan concerning how he received an impartation from a former saint who is now in Heaven.

> When I went on a three-day full fast (without food and water) in the early days of my ministry, on the third day of the fast I had a dream-like vision. I was not conscious whether I was awake or asleep. I was taken to a place where there were two mountains. Between the mountains were a valley and a huge building, which I understood represented the Church. Only the pillars were ready; the walls and other things were not up yet. The pillars were so big that you could drive three cars on them. High up on the building were some people I recognized. They were John Sung, Watchman Nee, and a few other people, some I recognized, and some I didn't. They had all gone to be with

the Lord and they were beckoning to me to go and join them.

I didn't know what it was, but in the spirit it was like I was going to them. And then I got out of this visitation. At that time I knew the two mountains represented the first and second coming. The pillars represented the pillars of prayer that build the church, the foundation. And these were men of God who had built some of these things. But a few years ago, God said to me: "Son, do you understand what that vision means?" I said, "No, Lord." The Lord said, "I have called you to continue the work which Watchmen Nee, John Sung, and the others have done. I have put an anointing on your life to do that work and I'm calling you to finish that which they have started." When I saw that, I wept. Of course, like everyone else, I said, "Lord, I will do your will, I just want to do your will. I don't seek for fame, I don't seek for fortune, and I don't seek for anything. I just want to do your will and then go home.

And then some time after that, Watchman Nee came in two dreams and talked with me and imparted something. Later on, when the Lord was teaching me about the anointing, I met Kathryn Khulman in the spirit world and she said some things to me and imparted something. As I progressed spiritually, I met different people and I said, "Lord, I don't understand these things theologically." But through time the Lord began to show me: This is the communion of the saints that still goes on. Now, I didn't ask for it, I didn't pursue it. I was just seeking God and praying, meditating on the Word. I didn't seek to meet anyone of them at all. But the Lord showed me that there were some things in their lives and their spirits that they had harnessed and gathered and imparted into my life in some way that my mind doesn't comprehend or understand.[2]

Dr. Tan's testimony helps us to realize that it is not necessary to physically meet someone in order to receive a mantle or impartation. Brother Tan never physically met Watchman Nee. Bob Jones never physically met the prophet from South Africa whose mantle he inherited. In my own life I never physically met the prophet whose mantle the Lord passed on to me. In my case, there's no natural way I could have met him since he lived hundreds of years before I was born. What's important to remember is that these former saints are still alive in Heaven, and as Brother Tan pointed out, there is still a communion of the saints taking place today.

Of course, many believers get a little bit nervous when you start talking along this line about having met someone who is dead. What they fail to realize is that these are visionary experiences that occur in the realm of the spirit, and these former saints are still alive spiritually. One of the best examples of this can be found in the Book of Revelation when the writer John encounters this type of situation:

*Then he said to me, "Write: 'Blessed are those who are called to the marriage supper of the Lamb!'" And he said to me, "These are the true sayings of God." And I fell at his feet to worship him. But he said to me, "See that you do not do that!* **I am your fellow servant, and of your brethren** *who have the testimony of Jesus. Worship God!* (Revelation 19:9-10)

Some translations attempt to make it sound like this person was a servant just like John's brethren. But the King James Version and the New King James Version translate it accurately by saying "of your brethren," denoting that he is also a Christian brother. This was not an angel that John was talking to. This was a fellow servant and Christian brother that had gone on to be with the Lord. Here we see John who was still alive on the earth having been caught up in a vision to Heaven and there carrying on a conversation with a redeemed saint. Why should we think this strange when we clearly find it in the New Testament? When Jesus walked on the earth as a man, He also had fellowship with saints who had previously left the earth.

> *Now after six days Jesus took Peter, James, and John his brother, led them up on a high mountain by themselves; and He was transfigured before them. His face shown like the sun, and His clothes became as white as the light. And behold, Moses and Elijah appeared to them, talking with Him* (Matthew 17:1-3).

Here we see Jesus talking with Moses and Elijah. Some people may think this a little bit far out, but it's there in the Bible and it won't go away. Please keep in mind that this meeting took place in the spirit realm. You would need to have the

90

gift of discerning of spirits in operation in order to see this. How do we know this took place in the spirit realm? The following verse proves it to be so.

> *Now as they came down from the mountain, Jesus commanded them, saying, "Tell the <u>vision</u> to no one until the Son of Man is risen from the dead* (Matthew 17:9).

Jesus, Peter, James, and his brother John, all at the same time **had a vision** while they were on that mountain. This was an open vision which allowed them to see with their natural eyes being wide open while at the same time seeing into the realm of the spirit with their spiritual eyes. During this vision they saw Jesus transfigured and Him talking with Moses and Elijah. This is a supernatural manifestation known in the Bible as the gift of discerning of spirits, which Paul spoke of in First Corinthians chapter 12.

## DISCERNING OF SPIRITS

What is the gift of discerning of spirits? Some people have misquoted the Word of God and call it the gift of discernment. But discernment in itself is not a gift. Discernment is the ability to accurately judge a matter. This in itself does not require a supernatural act of God. We all should use good judgment in the daily affairs of life. But the gift of discerning of spirits is different. The gift of discerning of spirits is a supernatural manifestation of the Holy Spirit that allows you to see, hear, taste, touch, and smell *in the realm of the spirit.*

Whenever a person experiences a vision, the gift of discerning of spirits is in operation. Actually, throughout the Old Testament, all the gifts of the Spirit, except for tongues and interpretation of tongues, were in operation. Tongues and interpretation of tongues are exclusive to this church-age dispensation. Today, all nine gifts of the Spirit that Paul spoke of in First Corinthians chapter 12 are in operation as the Spirit wills.

## THREE TYPES OF VISIONS

There are three types of visions that we see in Scripture. The first is known as an *open vision*. The experience the three apostles had on the mountain with Jesus was an open vision. An open vision is the highest type of vision. They not only *saw* Jesus transfigured but they also *heard* his conversation with Moses and Elijah. The Gospel of Luke gives us insight into what the discussion actually focused on, but that's a different topic for another time.

If you were to have stood on that mountain close by to see Jesus and the apostles when this event took place, you would not have noticed anything unusual **unless** the gift of discerning of spirits operated through you allowing you to enter into the same vision. In the natural, all you would have seen were three startled apostles and Jesus apparently saying something to someone you could not see. You can more readily see now why some issues that are truly biblical are very controversial to others because they have no understanding of the spirit realm nor how it operates.

I believe there are going to be times when whole groups of believers experience open visions simultaneously. It happened to Jesus, Peter, James, and John all at the same time. There will be times entire prayer groups will be caught up to the throne room to behold the glory of God through open visions. Entire children's classes in church will see angels. The supernatural is invading the Church. Christian leaders must have a solid biblical foundation to stand on as they lead in these coming waves of revival glory.

The second type of vision expressed in Scripture is what is known as a *trance*. In a trance, your physical senses are suspended and you are only aware of the spirit realm. We see this taking place in Peter's life when he went up on the housetop to pray. While there, a tremendous hunger for food came over him. This was not a result of having skipped breakfast, but it was the Spirit of God moving upon Peter, prepping him for a supernatural encounter that was about to take place.

> *Then he became very hungry and wanted to eat; but while they made ready, he fell into a trance* (Acts 10:10).

Notice Peter *fell* into a trance. This was not a self-induced experience that he brought on by himself. That's the difference between genuine manifestations of the Holy Spirit and occult and New Age practices. People in New Age practices can cause themselves to go into a trance. This is normal for them to do. For them, it's just as easy as pushing a button on a microwave oven. But Peter did not put himself into a trance. The Holy Spirit caused him to fall into a trance. Entering into the realm of the spirit any other way outside of the Holy Spirit is moving into the realm of occult powers. Don't push or try to make something supernatural happen. Demons force and coerce. The Holy Spirit leads us into experiences that we might more clearly know Jesus. The Holy Spirit glorifies Jesus, not experiences.

In his trance, Peter sees a large sheet lowered down to earth full of animals that were considered unclean according to Mosaic law. The Holy Spirit is beginning to open the eyes of Peter's understanding that the sacrificial death of Jesus was not only for the redemption of the Jews but also for all peoples of the world. It was just after this experience that Cornelius and his family and friends became the first Gentile converts to Christianity.

> *Now while Peter wondered within himself **what this vision which he had seen meant,** behold, the men who had been sent from Cornelius had made inquiry for Simon's house, and stood before the gate* (Acts 10:17).

> ***While Peter thought about the vision,*** *the Spirit said to him, "Behold, three men are seeking you* (Acts 10:19).

Here we see two times where the aforementioned trance is now identified as being a vision. A trance is one of the three types of visions. In my personal walk with the Lord I have noticed that the times when the Holy Spirit has come upon me and taken me to Heaven have most often been in a trance state of vision. In my book, *Working with Angels,* I describe how I was taken to Heaven and given a necklace called the *Diamond of Hope.* That experience actually took place when I fell into a trance when in a time of deep prayer. Open your heart to these types of experiences that the Holy Spirit grants. Jesus purchased these types of inheritances for us on the cross along with salvation and every other blessing.

The third type of vision is known as a *spiritual vision.* This is when your eyes are closed and you see an image—a vision— appear to you. This is what happened to Saul as he was going through his conversion experience. After having His encounter with the Lord on the road to Damascus he was left blinded by the Lord's brilliant glory.

> *Then Saul arose from the ground, and* **when his eyes were** **opened he saw no one.** *But they led him by the hand and brought him into Damascus. And he was* **three days with-** **out sight,** *and neither ate nor drank* (Acts 9:8-9).

We see from the above verse that Saul was in a condition of blindness. Keep that in mind as we examine the following verse.

> *Now there was a certain disciple at Damascus named Ana-* *nias; and to him the Lord said in a vision, "Ananias." And he said, "Here I am, Lord." So the Lord said to him, "Arise and go to the street called Straight, and inquire at the house of Judas for one called Saul of Tarsus, for behold, he is pray-* *ing.* **And in a vision he has seen** *a man named Ananias coming in and putting his hand on him, so that he might re-* *ceive his sight* (Acts 9:10-12).

Here we see that Saul has had a vision while in prayer. What's interesting to note is that this vision took place when he was blind. His natural eyesight had not yet been restored. It was restored later when Ananias prayed for Saul and something like scales fell from his eyes. But when he had the vision he was still blind. This would thus be considered a spiritual vision. In a spiritual vision, your eyes are closed and you see the vision within. In a spiritual vision your mind is involved. This is why we need to be careful what we allow our eyes to see and ears to hear. Spiritual pollution will *muddy the waters* and make it difficult to distinguish genuine Holy Spirit manifestations. Jesus said,

*The lamp of the body is the eye. Therefore, when your eye is good, your whole body is also full of light. But when your eye is bad, your body also is full of darkness* (Luke 11:34).

I have experienced open visions and trances numerous times but most of the visions I have are spiritual visions. I have found this to be the case across the board also with the majority of ministers I've spoken with. These are supernatural manifestations of the Holy Spirit. Of course, you can't push a button and make these types of things happen; it is only as the Holy Spirit wills. But I have discovered that the Holy Spirit is more willing then many have ever thought to reveal more and more of Jesus to us. As we position ourselves to walk near to God, the supernatural becomes a much more common experience and the mysteries of God are unfolded before us.

Another interesting event regarding encounters with redeemed saints who have gone on before can be found immediately following the Lord's resurrection. The fact that it was after the Lord's resurrection means this is a New Testament event.

*And Jesus cried out again with a loud voice, and yielded up His spirit. Then, behold, the veil of the temple was torn in two from top to bottom; and the earth quaked, and the rocks were split, and the graves were opened; and many bodies of the saints who had fallen asleep were raised; and coming out of the graves after His resurrection, **they went into the holy city and appeared to many*** (Matthew 27:50-53).

Here we have another verse referring to an event after the resurrection that shows communication between saints on the earth and those saints from the spirit realm who belong to the Lord. This event was not "far out" or heretical, but rather holy and glorious. The Scripture says, "they appeared to many." You can only imagine the excitement and awe that this would cause. What's remarkable about this particular event is that the saints who arose obviously walked around in physical bodies. Those who saw them did not have to experience a vision; it was fully manifested in the natural realm for all to see.

God's timing for this event couldn't have been better. The Jewish historian Josephus tells us there were more then a million visitors in Jerusalem. It was one of the cycle years when Jews made their pilgrimage from all over the world to make their sacrifices. The whole city was shaken to the foundation over the story of the Lord's empty tomb. Those redeemed saints who walked around brought witness to the Lord's resurrection. The Bible does not mention their names, but I could easily see Abraham, Joseph, Judah, Moses, Miriam, Samson, Ruth, David, and a host of other redeemed saints walking around alive in Jerusalem! What would you have done? You would probably do the same thing I would do—go up and talk to them!

Don't you think this event must have upset a lot of people's theology? I believe in good theology, but there are simply some things about God we are never going to understand. God is going to pour forth signs and wonders in His church today that are going to cause people's jaws to drop in amazement. If these things took place to give witness to the Lord's resurrection, just imagine what He will do to give witness to His Second Coming. Get ready. We haven't seen anything yet.

I love reading testimonies of saints who have had visions of Heaven and then come back to tell what they saw and who they met. When it's from the Lord it always blesses my heart. All of the former saints who have died and gone to Heaven are still there today. Jesus knew this very well and endeavored to help the Sadducees understand this truth.

> *But concerning the resurrection of the dead, have you not read what was spoken to you by God, saying, "I am the God of Abraham, the God of Isaac, and the God of Jacob"? God is not the God of the dead, but of the living* (Matthew 22:31-32).

Sometimes it is difficult fellowshipping with some Christians. They are so earthbound and carnally minded that sometimes you just want to hook up with somebody who is spiritually deep. As a minister I have to come down from the mountaintop to help others who are weak and cannot climb the mountain of God on their own. But there are times when I want to be on that mountaintop with somebody so we together can just shout and praise God until we've gotten it out of our systems! I believe that's why the Lord has allowed me to have supernatural encounters in the glory realm. The writer of the Book of Hebrews understood this realm:

*But you have come to Mount Zion and to the city of the living God, the heavenly Jerusalem, to an innumerable company of angels, to the general assembly and church of the firstborn who are registered in heaven, to God the Judge of all, **to the spirits of just men made perfect,** to Jesus the Mediator of the new covenant, and to the blood of sprinkling that speaks better things than that of Abel* (Hebrews 12:22-24).

The phrase, "But you **have come** to Mount Zion" (see Heb. 12:22) denotes that as believers in Christ we have arrived, not that we are still on the journey and someday hope to get there. In Mount Zion are the spirits of just men made perfect. Their *bodies* are not there (except for Enoch and Elijah) but their *spirits* are. One day the saints in Heaven will all receive glorified bodies along with every other saint who is alive today. This will take place at the resurrection of the dead and all saints will be clothed in a new, glorified body that is imperishable. The saints now in Heaven have not yet received their glorified *bodies,* except for Jesus. Jesus has received His glorified body; it is not in a grave. His grave is empty. After His resurrection, Jesus received His glorified body and appeared to the apostles as a man in a body, not as a spirit without a body.

*And He said to them, "Why are you troubled? And why do doubts arise in your hearts? Behold My hands and My feet, that it is I Myself. Handle Me and see, for a spirit does not have flesh and bones as you see I have"* (Luke 24:38-39).

Notice Jesus said *flesh and bones* and not *flesh and blood.* His blood was poured out at Calvary for our sins. His blood in His glorified body was poured on the mercy seat in Heaven upon His ascension. On His way to accomplish this, He revealed Himself to Mary next to the empty tomb. When Mary saw Jesus, she was so emotionally charged that she clung to Him like glue. Jesus responded to her by saying:

> *Do not cling to Me, for I have not yet ascended to My Father...* (John 20:17).

## JESUS AS HIGH PRIEST

The high priest in the Old Testament would go into the Most Holy Place of the tabernacle once a year to sprinkle blood on the Mercy Seat to atone for the sins of the people. It would not wash away their sins—it could only cover them on an annual basis that had to be repeated over and over again.

Jesus came as High Priest into the Most Holy Place in the heavenly tabernacle and presented His blood; not the blood of bulls or goats—but His own blood. This one redemptive act repaired man's separation from God once and for all. Through Christ, we have now come to Mount Zion. This is why He told Mary not to cling to Him. He was on His way to Heaven to present Himself before His Father as the High Priest of humanity. Once that was taken care of, He allowed certain people to touch Him during the forty days He spent on earth between His resurrection and His ascension to the Father's right hand.

Those who have been purchased with the blood of the Lamb belong to the Church of the living God. The Church in Heaven and the Church on earth are one Church. The Church is not divided in two, with half in Heaven and the other half on earth. We are one Church—one family.

> *For this reason I bow my knees to the Father of our Lord Jesus Christ, from whom the **whole family in heaven and earth** is named* (Ephesians 3:14-15).

This is why there may be special times when God allows a person on earth to come in contact in the spirit realm with the spirit of a just man (or woman) who has been made perfect. Countless people have met the Lord Jesus Christ through visions. Countless others have seen angels through visionary experiences, at times even conversing with them. Throughout the centuries of Church history there are countless stories as well of Christians on the earth who encountered a redeemed saint through a vision.

A lot of people throw up a red flag on topics such as this and quickly label it necromancy.

> *There shall not be found among you anyone who makes his son or daughter pass through the fire, or one who practices witchcraft, or a soothsayer, or one who interprets omens, or a sorcerer, or one who conjures spells, or a medium, or a spiritist, or one who calls up the dead* (Deuteronomy 18:10-11).

The practice of necromancy is calling up the spirit of the dead. The most famous instance we see of this is of Saul and the medium of Endor found in First Samuel chapter 28. The practice of consulting the dead was common among the heathen nations. It's still very popular today in New Age and psychic groups. What these people do not understand is that in reality, they **are not** communicating with the dead. They are communicating with familiar spirits.

What are familiar spirits? A familiar spirit is an evil spirit that is familiar with someone. Demons know information about people, even the people of God. They may know your name, the address of where you live, and can even imitate certain mannerisms of the person that are consistent with an individual's personality. When a medium practices calling up the dead, she is in reality coming in contact with a familiar spirit. This is strictly forbidden in Scripture.

When someone dies he or she goes to either one of two places. They either go to Heaven if they belong to Christ, or they go to hell if they belong to the devil. You cannot call up dead people from hell to speak with them. Even if you could call them up, you wouldn't be able to get anything useful out of them due to them being on fire and suffering the indescribable torments of hell. Of course, somebody is wondering, *If this is true, then how was the medium of Endor able to call up Samuel upon the request of King Saul?* That's a good question. If you read that text carefully, you will see that it was definitely the real Samuel who spoke. Mediums believe they are truly making contact with the dead, but they fail to understand they have yielded themselves to demonic, evil spirits who share with them supernatural information. Just because it is supernatural doesn't mean it is from God! That fools a lot of people.

What transpired was that the medium got the shock of her life when the Holy Spirit moved into the situation during the séance. King Saul had come to this woman at night and disguised himself.

> *Then the woman said, "Whom shall I bring up for you?" And he said, "Bring up Samuel for me"* (1 Samuel 28:11).

Normally this woman would then conjure up the dead and a familiar spirit would accommodate her. The spirit that would be familiar with the dead person would then speak through this woman using the woman's vocal chords. The familiar spirit would sound and talk like the deceased person, thus making it seem from all appearances that the dead person had been contacted.

> *When the woman saw Samuel, she cried out with a loud voice. And the woman spoke to Saul saying, "Why have you deceived me? For you are Saul!"* (1 Samuel 28:12).

The Spirit of God showed up at the séance! The medium became terrified, but Saul assured her she wouldn't die. Samuel then speaks to Saul and through a brief message tells Saul that because of his rebellion against the Word of God he has lost the kingdom and he would be dead by the next day. Of course, an interesting question here is how exactly did Samuel speak to Saul? The Bible doesn't clearly say. Keep in mind that the Spirit of God came upon the medium and she had a vision of Samuel. Saul did not see Samuel because he did not have the vision. How then did he hear Samuel? Most likely he heard Samuel speak through the woman's voice.

If persons yield their voices to the devil, then it is possible for demons to speak through these individuals using their vocal chords. Likewise, the Holy Spirit can speak through an individual who yields his or her voice to Him, and speak forth the inspired utterance. This is known as the gift of prophecy. Somebody may say, "God would never speak through a witch!" However, it appears from the above text that the Holy Spirit caused Samuel to speak through the medium. God can speak through anybody he wants to, even a donkey. I sometimes think it's easier for God to speak through a donkey than some people who are so adamantly opposed to anything that's outside of their circle of biblical understanding.

Dr. John G. Lake once had an experience along this same line when he was praying for a woman with a severe eye injury. As he was praying, the Spirit of the Lord came upon the woman and completely healed her eye. Then Dr. Lake said the Holy Spirit allowed his former wife who had died on the mission field to speak through this woman's voice.[3] Someone may say, "That's of the devil." Well, if it's of the devil, then why did the message given through the woman glorify God and why was the woman's eye healed? There is a true spiritualism that runs very deep that many are completely unaware of. With the Word of God as our foundation and the Holy Spirit as our guide we can discern the true from the false and not be in fear of the unknown realms of spiritual truth.

I'd like to share an interesting note about the medium of Endor. This woman lived in Endor, which is a town located in Issachar but assigned to Manasseh's possession. This town can still be seen today about four miles south of Mount Tabor. This woman practiced in the occult and was enslaved to spiritual darkness. Unless she repented and turned from her sins to God, she would have died and gone to hell. There's something I've noticed about many of these people in New Age and psychic groups that can be observed. There's no question that many of them are "gifted" by having an inclination toward things that are spiritual. The only problem is that they are deceived by the devil and they operate in the kingdom of darkness. Why do many of these people have such a strong attraction to the spiritual realm? The answer—because many of them are called to the prophetic ministry and they don't know it.

I've seen it over and over again. A dear friend of mine who has a powerful prophetic ministry went to Scotland several years ago. His ancestry is Scottish of which he and his parents are very proud. While there in Scotland, he thought he would research his family genealogy, perhaps thinking he would discover that he was related to the former kings that ruled Scotland. Imagine his surprise when he discovered through well-kept books of ancient family lineage that for generations his family members were all witches! See, his family lineage just had that calling to the spirit realm. They were "wired" and drawn towards the supernatural. What does the Bible say about this?

> *For the gifts and the calling of God are irrevocable* (Romans 11:29).

Once God bestows a gift it is freely given and He doesn't change His mind at a later time. Due to a lack of understanding, many of those in histories past who were called as prophets were not received or understood. Often they were labeled as witches and warlocks, when in reality they were God's chosen vessels. Such was the case with Joan of Arc who was a prophetess and seer but was labeled a witch. This was also true of King Arthur and his well-known wizard, Merlin. The truth is that Merlin was actually the King's prophet, but he got labeled a wizard by medieval historians who viewed miracles and all supernatural phenomena as being of the devil.

## GENERATIONAL BLESSINGS

A call to a ministry office is also a calling that usually runs down the family line. The children might not accept it but it is available nonetheless. This calling can run unbroken for generations because of an original covenant of blessing that someone made with the Lord. We hear a lot of teaching on generational curses and this teaching can help certain people overcome troubling barriers consisting of bad habits and addictions. However, I choose to focus much more highly on generational blessings, which unfortunately we hear much less teaching on.

The majority of those who are known as popular rock and pop musicians are called by God to be worship leaders. Many who are on the street running drugs and organizing vast networks of complex drug trafficking that net millions of dollars are called to the apostolic ministry. Without Christ, people don't understand their gifting or their purpose. We must help them fulfill their destiny that can only be understood through salvation in the Lord Jesus Christ.

**Padre Pio (1887-1968) and Maria Esperanza**—Padre Pio is one of those saints whose life I always greatly enjoy reading about. Although unknown to many in the western Church, his life and ministry were still a blessing to thousands around the world. He seemed to somehow have one foot in the heavenly realm, which enabled him to connect with God, and the other foot in the earth realm, which allowed him to take care of necessary everyday ministry work.

As a humble Capuchin priest from San Giovanni Rotondo, Italy, he was chosen by God as a prophet and anointed with a ministry full of signs and wonders. Beautiful heavenly fragrances would often be released as Padre Pio ministered in the power of the Holy Spirit. The gift of prophecy and the gift of the word of knowledge operated with purity and accuracy throughout his long ministry. Many sick people were miraculously healed through his prayers, often of incurable diseases. There were even times when Padre Pio was carried away and translated to different locations by the Holy Spirit, just as Philip was in the book of Acts after he had baptized the Ethiopian eunuch. (See Acts 8:39.) However, Padre Pio was most widely known for the bleeding wounds in his hands, feet, and side that stayed with him for fifty years. These wounds, known as stigmata, were not a sickness nor a disease, but rather a supernatural sign and wonder pointing people to salvation in Christ Jesus. Padre Pio shared that when he first received these wounds in 1918, it caused him great embarrassment and humiliation, much like what Jesus felt and experienced while hanging on the cross as He suffered the rejection of men.[4]

There is such a thing as stigmata. That is when a person so deeply contemplates on something that it actually becomes a reality in his or her own life. Along with Padre Pio, another good example of this would be Saint Francis of Assisi. He contemplated the Cross of Christ with such intensity and was so moved by it that he said to his followers, "When I am dead, open my body, and you will find the impress of the Cross of Christ on my heart." Sure enough, after his death they opened his body and there was the impress of the Cross of Christ on his heart. Saint Francis also experienced stigmata in his hands, feet, and side.

> *I will show wonders in the heaven above and **signs on the earth below, blood** and fire and billows of smoke* (Acts 2:19 NIV).

> *From now on let no one trouble me, **for I bear in my body the marks of the Lord Jesus*** (Galatians 6:17).

Some will say these marks that Paul is speaking of refer to the scars and marks left by the countless beatings and scourgings he suffered. While I'm sure this could be viewed as the primary application of this Scripture, I have also found the Word of God to be multi-layered. Before his salvation experience, Paul had murdered innocent people in his fanatical zeal for Judaism. Upon his acceptance of the Lord Jesus into his life, his sins were washed away by the Lord's blood. I'm sure Paul focused often on the Lord's blood and its marvelous cleansing power. He had to remind himself often that he was totally forgiven. Catholic tradition teaches that this Scripture also refers to Paul experiencing stigmata at times due to his meditating on the cleansing blood of Christ while "forgetting those things which are behind and reaching forward to those things which are ahead" (Phil. 3:13). The blood of Christ washes away our past sins and failures.

Padre Pio experienced the stigmata until just before he died at the age of 81. My point here is not to focus on stigmata but rather on the transfer of a remarkable mantle. However, in regard to the stigmata, I would suggest that believers focus on the ascended Christ and not see the Lord as One who is continually on the cross. He's not on the cross anymore. He ascended to Heaven, and today He is seated at the right hand of God the Father in majesty. If a person can focus on the blood cleansing power of the cross and, through that deep meditation, experience stigmata of bleeding hands and feet, just imagine what kind of manifestations could be experienced when we constantly see ourselves as being seated with Christ Jesus in the heavenly places.

Maria Esperanza from Venezuela is anointed of the Lord as a prophet and seer. Widely known for her healing ministry and accurate prophetic words, her ministry is one of the most documented miracle ministries in the world. When Padre Pio was an aged man, he was quoted as having told others an extraordinary woman would soon visit him. "There is a young woman who is going to come from South America. When I leave, she will be your consolation."

Maria was led of the Spirit to travel to San Giovanni Rotondo, Italy to meet Padre Pio. Upon arriving, there were throngs of people wanting to see Padre Pio, but, knowing in the spirit that his special visitor had just arrived, he cried out, "Esperanza!"

On September 23, 1968, Maria had a vision of Padre Pio. "Esperanza," he said in the vision, "I have come to say good-bye. My time has come. It is your turn." The next day, Maria and her husband saw in the newspaper that Padre Pio (whose funeral would be attended by more than a million people) had died. Maria's life and miracle ministry bear a remarkable resemblance to the godly man whose mantle she inherited. Her close walk with God has manifested a life of unusual signs and wonders. There have been times when friends have volunteered to wash and dry her clothes to help free her up that she might have more time in prayer. Often when pulling her clothes out of the dryer, they would discover that hundreds of fresh rose petals had appeared in the dryer![5]

In looking at these examples of mantles that were passed from one individual to another, there is a very important truth that I want you to see. This truth is that when a ministry is birthed by God, it is always His desire to see this type of ministry remain in the earth until the Lord returns. The individual that God started the ministry through can only remain for a limited time before his or her life on earth is complete. The Lord is looking for men and women who will be willing to take up the mantle that God has for them and run the course that He has charted for their lives.

**Sadhu Sundar Singh (1889-1929) and Sadhu Sundar Selvaraj**—Sadhu Sundar Singh was India's foremost Christian "Sadhu" ("Sadhu" means teacher) of the early 20th century. Brother Singh was a man much like Enoch who walked very close to the Lord. He was affectionately known around the world as the "apostle of the bleeding feet," because the soles of his feet were often covered in bloody blisters from all the walking he did while spreading the Gospel.

Sundar Singh was raised a devout Sikh, and was consecrated from his youth to become a Hindu Sadhu. His mother admonished him to become a Hindu Sadhu, saying, "Do not be selfish and materialistic like your brothers, but seek for your peace of mind and hold steadily onto your faith. Be a sadhu." From the age of seven and onward Sundar Singh devoured the teachings of the Sikh and Hindu teachers. He learned the Hindu teachings of yoga, mastered Vedas (the ancient Hindu teachings) and also studied the Qur'an. He was often taken by his mother into the rainforest to be instructed by a Hindu Sadhu. Yet having studied so diligently he still felt a great lack of inward peace which he hoped his religion would offer.

Sundar's mother died when he was 14 years old. This was very difficult for him. His mother had previously placed him in a school run by British missionaries. It was here that he was first exposed to the Bible. Upon his mother's death he reached a great despair, often reflected in angry outbursts. He publicly tore and burned a Bible page by page, and even threw stones at local missionaries and preachers. He even contemplated suicide, hoping that he would somehow find true peace through the Hindu teaching of reincarnation.

Shortly after he had burned the Bible, he awoke at 3:00 A.M. for his ritualistic bath in the courtyard observed by devoted Hindus and Sikhs. Upon returning to his room he had a dramatic encounter with the Lord Jesus Christ through a vision. The experience was so overwhelming it completely changed his life. He had finally discovered the source of all true peace and joy. Brother Singh dedicated his heart fully to the Lord. Despite tremendous opposition from his father and family members he was soon baptized and became a Christian Sadhu.

Brother Singh wisely chose to make his lifestyle identical to the Hindu Sadhus of his day, including the same style of dress, spiritual discipline, and method of teaching in order to relate to the Indian people. However, unlike the Hindu Sadhus, he refused to allow himself to become dirty and was very neat and clean, and he did not torture his body with the ascetic rituals that Hindu Sadhus practiced.

Despite suffering tremendous persecution for preaching Christ, Brother Singh always prayed for his enemies and he blessed those who cursed him. Men who knew him said he was more like Christ than any other man they had known.

Each day Brother Singh would spend two hours reading the Word of God, meditating on the Word of God, and praying. On certain days he would pray all day long. Often, during times of prayer and meditation of the Scriptures, he would enter into visions and would be caught up into Heaven. This occurred more frequently during the latter years of his ministry, often as much as ten times a month. Concerning these experiences he said:

"I never try to go into ecstasy; nor do I advise others to try. It is a gift to be accepted, but it should not be sought; if given, it is a pearl of great price."[6]

Brother Singh's encounters with the Lord through the visions he experienced relate the glories and wonders of Heaven, and answer many questions regarding God's plan for man. In his book titled, *At the Master's Feet,* Brother Singh shares with us the messages the Lord gave to him during his visions.[7] The lessons shared by the Lord were given to Brother Singh in the traditional Asian style of teaching, which is in the form of parables, and this style is still prevalent in many parts of the world today.

Brother Singh's ministry work eventually took him to Europe and America. Wherever the Lord led him to minister, many people were drawn to hear his revelatory Bible teaching. While in Europe, a young teenage girl named Corrie Ten Boom (from the World War II story of *The Hiding Place*), wanted so badly to hear Sundar Singh minister that she came to his conference with a blanket and was prepared to sleep out in a field. God intervened and a kind student found a room for her. Corrie was deeply touched as she heard Brother Singh's testimony of how he had seen the Lord Jesus during his conversion experience when he became a Christian. This disturbed her that as a Christian she had never seen a vision of Christ nor performed miracles. She met Sadhu Singh on a walk and was able to ask him why this never happened to her. Sundar responded that *she* was the real miracle. He believed in Christ only *after* seeing Him. On the other hand, she had simply heard and believed.[8] He then quoted to her the words of Christ:

*Jesus said to him, "Thomas, because you have seen Me, you have believed. Blessed are those who have not seen and yet have believed"* (John 20:29).

Just as God delivered Brother Singh from the deception of false religion and gave him a worldwide ministry, it was also God's plan to continue this apostolic work after Brother Singh went to be with the Lord. In similar fashion, God called a young man named Sadhu Sundar Selvaraj out of Hinduism into the light of Truth. Brother Sadhu, as he is now affectionately known, gave his life to the Lord at the age of 16 after hearing a Christian teacher of science talk about the differences between the Theory of Evolution and the Creation account as told in the Bible. The work that God had planned for Brother Sadhu to accomplish would be revealed to him at the age of 21 through an encounter with the Lord Jesus Christ. His account of this experience is recorded as follows:

> On December 24, 1983, Brother Sadhu had a supernatural visitation from the Lord Jesus Christ. The Lord Jesus Christ appeared to him in the Spirit and began speaking to him about the legendary Sadhu Sundar Singh and the Sadhu's ministry in Tibet. The Lord Jesus spoke to him for about twenty minutes. The Lord Jesus then asked Sunder Selvaraj, "Will you continue that ministry?" Without any hesitation, Selvaraj answered "Yes Lord!" Smiling, the Lord said, "Do not reply hastily! This is a very difficult ministry with lots of suffering. You may have to suffer loneliness, isolation, hunger, pain, and persecutions. Now tell Me. Will you accept this ministry?" Humbly kneeling before the Lord Jesus, Selvaraj answered, "Yes Lord. I will continue Sadhu Sundar Singh's ministry."

Pleased with that answer, the Lord Jesus came towards Selvaraj and placed a mantle on him. Laying his hands upon him, the Lord Jesus then said, "I am ordaining you as an apostle to Tibet. Go and evangelize Tibet and her people. From today you shall be called Sadhu Sundar Selvaraj.

After two years of praying and waiting on God, the Lord Jesus revealed a strategy for the systematic evangelization of the Tibetans. Since 1986 Brother Sadhu has been going regularly to Tibet every year to bring God's love to the Tibetans.[9]

It is interesting to note the similarities between Brother Sadhu and the prophet Elisha whom we studied earlier. The Lord never wants someone to rush into something without that person knowing what he or she is getting into. I believe the Lord does this because He is not only looking for obedience, but also is looking for a willing heart. It's one thing to do what God said, but it's another thing to do it under difficult circumstances and maintain a positive attitude. God spoke the following statement through the mouth of Isaiah the prophet concerning this:

> *If you are willing and obedient, you will eat the best from the land* (Isaiah 1:19 NIV).

Some people are *obedient* to do what God instructs them to do, but they lag on the *willingness*. The Lord will only transfer mantles to those who are both willing *and* obedient. By His grace we are going to please the Lord in every area of our lives and do whatever He asks of us with a joyful and thankful heart!

115

The examples we have looked at of mantles being transferred and ministries being supernaturally continued in the earth are just a few of the many that take place in the Kingdom of God. Are you willing to receive the mantle that God has for you? Will you be obedient to follow the leading of the Holy Spirit? If yes, then be prepared because you are now standing on the front line to receive your mantle from Heaven.

## ENDNOTES

1. The story of Bob Jones' angelic encounter is used by permission. Bob Jones and Paul Keith Davis White Dove Ministries www.bobjones.org.

2. The article by Peter Tan is used by permission. Eagle Vision Website http://www.eaglevision.com.my/txttestimony.htm.

3. The story of John G. Lake is referenced from; *John G. Lake—His Life, His Sermons, His Boldness of Faith;* pages 132-133. Copyright 1994 Kenneth Copeland Publications Fort Worth, TX 76192-0001; www.kcm.org.

4. Editorial, "The 462nd Saint, The True Signifigance of Saint Pio of Pietrelcina" by Reverend Father Nicholas Mary, C.SS.R.

5. An overview of the life of Maria Esperanza can be found at http://www.spiritdaily.org/Prophecy-seers/Esperanza/Esperanza_story.htm.

6. The article of Sadhu Sundar Selvaraj's vision is used by permission. Jesus Ministries http://www.jesusministries .org/tibetan_2.html.

7. *At the Master's Feet* by Sadhu Sundar Singh is public domain. Translated from the Urdu by Rev. Arthur and Mrs. Parker Fleming H. Revell Company London and Edinburgh, 1922.

8. Corrie Ten Boom, *Clippings From My Notebook,* Fleming H. Revell, a division of Baker Book House Company.

# CHAPTER 7

# *Making the Most of a Mantle*

Of course, we understand that even when a person receives a mantle, that does not guarantee a person will be a success. Much has to do with work ethic and his or her level of devotion to the Lord. For instance, you could be a very gifted athlete with great natural ability. However, that natural talent and gifting by itself is not enough to make it to the very top. An athlete must train hard and put in the effort necessary to win. I've seen several guys who never lifted a barbell in their life and never worked out in a gym, yet they still had outstanding muscular development due to great genetics inherited through their family line. As blessed by the Lord as they are, they could still never measure up to someone who competes in a top caliber bodybuilding competition. Those guys who compete professionally in that realm have great genetics *plus* an incredible work ethic that places them on an entirely different level.

Having come from a competitive sports background, I can relate when it comes to training and preparation. All through high school and college I competed in track and field as a middle distance runner and enjoyed modest success. While in college I had a desire to study martial arts, so I joined a Tae Kwon Do school that was taught by a Korean Master Instructor.

After college I continued to train in Tae Kwon Do and, with a lot of hard work, I became fairly good at it. Soon I began competing in tournaments all over my home state of Texas and other states as well. In order to better prepare myself for competition, I would cross-train with other martial artists who practiced different styles. Often I would spar with those who trained in Karate, Judo, Kung Fu, Jiu Jitsu, and Aikido. Although my primary discipline was Tae Kwon Do, I would still compete in other tournaments to better develop my overall skills. Once I even competed in the Karate World Championships in the Men's Black Belt Division.

Even today, as a minister, I will cross train with any Christian who can share more insight about the Lord and help me walk closer with Him. To me, it doesn't matter if you are Pentecostal, Baptist, Lutheran, Methodist, Episcopalian, Catholic, Seventh Day Adventist, or whatever. No single person or denomination has all the truth. We can all learn from each other because we all make up the Body of Christ.

Having learned from other martial artists outside of my particular group proved to be very useful. One of my best sparring partners was well skilled in Karate and he was very good with his hands. Training with him increased my punching skills as well. Little did I know that the day would come when I would have to put these skills to use in a life-threatening situation.

It happened back in 1992, late one night when I was leaving a weekly prayer meeting in Lubbock, Texas. It was about 11 P.M. and I was escorting one of the lady church members to her car when an armed man approached us in the church parking lot and said, "Get in the car! We're going to go for a little ride!" Well, it didn't take a genius to figure out that this ride would be a one-way trip with no survivors. The young lady I was escorting totally froze up in fear and couldn't speak a single word! However, the Spirit of the Lord came upon me and with authority I said, "We're not going anywhere with you!" He said, "Get in the car now, or I'm going to blow you away!" When he said that, someone about 50 feet away in the distance walked by on the sidewalk and it was enough to distract him for a split second. Instantly with my right hand I reached low to block his gun while with my left hand I summoned all my strength and struck him with full force right in the center of the nose. The force of the impact immediately broke his nose and sent him flying backward up against the side of the wall of the church building. Although staggering and bloody from his broken nose, he still put up a pretty good fight because he was wired on drugs and seemed to possess demonic strength. Nevertheless, with the Lord's help, that scoundrel went down and he went down hard.

By this time, the young lady who had frozen up in fear was able to call for help. When the men of the church caught word of it, they rushed outside, but by then it was all over.

Of course, please understand that I am a man of peace, but in a life-threatening situation you must protect yourself and others. It's been many years now since I have completely laid down martial arts in order to follow the Lord in the spiritual art of Christ-like development. Even my collection of trophies and medals I threw away to signify my desire to go on in the things of God. The Lord melted out of me any desire to engage in any form of competition. Now I desire to do as Paul said and, "*Honor one another above yourselves*" (Rom. 12:10 NIV). I'm now looking forward to the day that Isaiah prophesied of saying:

> *He will judge between the nations and will settle disputes for many peoples. They will beat their swords into plowshares and their spears into pruning hooks. Nation will not take up sword against nation, **nor will they train for war anymore***
> (Isaiah 2:4 NIV).

Since that night, the only fight I have ever been in has been the *fight of faith* (see 1 Tim. 6:12). I don't even fight the devil. Jesus already defeated the devil at Calvary through His death, burial, and resurrection; therefore, I refuse to fight a defeated foe. Each day I put the Word of God into my heart so that my faith is strong enough to overwhelm all doubt and unbelief.

Putting Scriptures that are fresh and living into my heart through study and meditation enables me to walk with confidence in God, knowing that I am prepared to walk in victory throughout each day. The apostle Paul told Timothy to:

*Be diligent to present yourself approved to God, a worker who does not need to be ashamed, rightly dividing the word of truth* (2 Timothy 2:15).

We should take this business of being spiritually prepared for life seriously so that we will not be ashamed on our Day of Judgment. Some people will be embarrassed before God on the day they give account for the way they lived their lives. Don't wait until you get to Heaven before diving into the things of God. When you get to Heaven, your eternal rank will be set. Prepare now so that you can rejoice on that day. Don't squander away your precious time.

When I used to compete in martial arts tournaments, it was normal for my master instructor to put me through two-hour workouts. Sometimes on Saturdays the training sessions would last four to six hours. We would do thousands of pushups on our knuckles (on a concrete floor) and practice sparring techniques continually. It was necessary to do this because in many top-level tournaments it was not uncommon to see individuals carried off on stretchers because they got K.O.'d (Knocked Out). We trained hard so that we could perform well when we competed. We wanted our martial arts school to be represented well and we greatly desired to honor our instructor by doing our best when we competed.

I thank God I never lost any teeth or got knocked out, but I did get my bell rung pretty good a few times. Once I got my nose broken in a tournament through a spinning back-kick by a very talented Korean fighter. In another tournament I received a jolting roundhouse kick to the head that caused a hairline fracture in my jaw. After that kick, I couldn't chew or eat for a week because of the pain. Once in a sparring session I received a devastating punch from a Karate Black Belt right into my diaphragm. I never lost consciousness, but I couldn't get up off the floor for several minutes. There were lots of bruises and hurts, but at the same time I was receiving pain, I was certainly dishing some out as well.

My old Korean master instructor said I had one of the fastest skipping side-kicks he had ever seen. Above average speed coupled with all the years of running track through high school and college gave me great endurance and stamina. When a lot of the guys began to tire in competition, I would still feel fine. I would begin to pull ahead on points and score the most after several rounds when the competition would begin to fatigue. It was then that I would start using the skipping side-kick. After a while, my instructor told me to stop using it because I was breaking too many people's ribs just by that one kicking technique.

Well, I share these things as a natural example because we need to be prepared for the spiritual challenges we face in life. Many believers are content just to cruise through life and maybe read their Bible for about five minutes once every week. Well, five minutes is better than nothing at all, but a person is not going to progress very far moving at a snail's pace. There should be a fervency concerning spending time with God through prayer and the study of the Word. The more a person gives to this, the more he or she will be transformed into the image of Christ. When faced with distracting issues in the early Church, the twelve apostles responded by saying:

*But we will give ourselves continually to prayer, and to the ministry of the word* (Acts 6:4 KJV).

A Christian who receives a mantle must be devoted to the Lord in prayer and spend time studying the Word. Some Christians have already received mantles but time will tell whether or not they make the most of them. One particular case concerning this comes to my mind.

While ministering in a revival service in Hacienda Heights, California, I preached a faith-building message and then proceeded to minister to those in the meeting who desired prayer. One young lady in her early twenties came up and stood before me to receive prayer and prophetic ministry. As I began to pray for her, I sensed in my spirit a ministry calling upon her life. Operating through the gift of prophecy, I told her I believed that God had a calling upon her life into the ministry. She looked at me and smiled and said she was currently attending a local Bible college in order to prepare for the ministry. As I continued to pray, the Lord had me stop and ask her what her name was. She told me that Francine was her name. At that point the Spirit of the Lord moved upon me strongly and I said, "Just as your name is Francine, the same Holy Spirit that was upon Saint Francis of

Assisi is upon you. And you will write as he did and your writings will bless many!"

## WALK IN YOUR MANTLE

When I said that her eyes got as big as saucers and she said, "I'll be right back." She quickly returned after having gone to the other side of the church to retrieve something from her mother who was in the service. In her hand was a two-page poem that she had just written two nights earlier in which she had poured out her heart to God. She had only shared this writing with her mother and was planning on making a book out of her writings when she had enough material. Several days after the meeting, I received in the mail a copy of the spiritual poem which she had written. It was very much anointed and a blessing to read. The question now is will she fulfill her calling and walk in the mantle that the Lord has so graciously bestowed upon her? Remember, once the mantle comes, then it is time to go to work. Rejoice when you receive your mantle, but don't stop there. Step through every door that God opens for you and make the most of every opportunity.

We are living in a time when Heaven and earth are merging together. Expect help from the other side as Heaven draws near. The gifted mystic saint John Wright Follette wrote;

> I feel there is an invasion of God all the time. I feel it
> in the world; I feel like He is pushing in all the time. I
> feel that toward the end of this time, Heaven is push-
> ing toward the earth in its last struggle. I feel it in my

spirit; that invasion; that push; that holy urge of God. Some spirits become conscious of it, and are quite overwhelmed with it. They should be. Others are not, and I am very charitable with them.[1]

That heavenly invasion is here and mantles are being given to the Church to walk in end-time authority and power in Christ.

Recently I was ministering at a conference when a wonderful experience took place. I was on the front row during the time of praise and worship for the night service. I was scheduled to speak that night following the praise and worship. During the singing to the Lord I got so caught up in the spirit that I went into a vision. It was a moment of total spiritual ecstasy. In this vision I saw the Lord walk into the church building and come and stand by my side on the front row. He smiled at me, making me feel very comfortable in His presence. As He came into the building, He also had someone else with Him. It was Joan of Arc.

If you are not familiar with Joan of Arc, then let me share with you that she was a young woman that God used to save France from being taken over by the English during the 100 Year War. She was born in France in 1412 and at the age of twelve she began having visitations by angels and redeemed saints who encouraged her to do the will of God and help deliver France. These experiences took place through visions in which Joan was given supernatural guidance that always proved accurate. She accepted her calling and did help France overthrow the English in astonishing victories that she led against impossible odds. However, she was eventually taken captive by the English. A mock trial was ordered to try her on charges of witchcraft and heresy. There was not a shred of real evidence against her, but because the trial was politically motivated, Joan was falsely accused and condemned. She was burned at the stake at the age of nineteen. Twenty-four years later, Pope Callixtus III reopened her case and with irrefutable evidence proved that Joan was completely innocent of all charges.[2]

As the Lord walked over and stood next to me, Joan of Arc had walked to the other side of the church sanctuary and stood next to a woman whom I met just the previous day. This woman had flown into town to attend the conference. She was a fellow minister of the Gospel who lived in a different state. About the only thing I knew about this woman was her name and that she was a minister from out of state, but no other personal information. I watched as Joan of Arc looked at the Lord to get a confirming nod that she was standing next to the right person. The Lord gave a nod with His head that indicated, "Yes." She also looked at me and smiled. This redeemed saint was radiant and the glory of God was all over her. Her golden-brown hair came down to her shoulders and she wore a beautiful white robe with gold embroidery. She seemed to be almost transparent, as if she were made of light.

That night I taught the Word of God for about an hour before I began to minister in the Holy Spirit. As I moved into the time of ministry in the spirit, I told this woman, in front of all those attending the conference, that a Joan of Arc anointing was being placed upon her life. I then prayed over her and spoke a blessing over her life.

After the conference was over, I was relaxing in a back room, fellowshipping with the director who was in charge of the video recording for the conference. This kind man was a brother in the Lord who has a team that travels all over America and does live audio and video recording for Christian conferences. He shared with me how just a few months earlier in the year he was recording a conference for the woman that I had just ministered to prophetically. He said my prophetic word was right on. He told me he had personally recorded her conference and the theme for it was, "The Joan of Arc Anointing."

## THE JOAN OF ARC ANOINTING

What is a Joan of Arc anointing? It is an anointing to die to your own desires at an early age and thus touch the nations with an uncompromising stand for the Gospel. Many people are receiving a portion of this mantle. Before the second coming of the Lord, every mantle that has ever been bestowed by the Spirit of God throughout church history will rest upon the end-time Church.

Again we see a mantle being released. Once a mantle is received, then it means added responsibility. There will never be a substitute for good, hard work. I know the mantles that the Lord has placed upon my life. But don't think for a minute that I just walk out and start ministering and don't spend any time in prayer or Bible study. You can't build a ministry on just a gift or a testimony. Those who try to do that will fail in the long-run. I've committed to build the ministry the Lord has given me on preaching and teaching the Word of God. Signs and wonders follow the Word. Everything works great when you put the Word first.

A very dear friend of mine is a world class composer and symphony conductor. He has studied music all his life and knew at the age of four that he would be a composer and conductor. He has currently written a beautiful oratorio that puts certain biblical chapters to music, much like what Handel did with the masterpiece known as "The Messiah." This friend of mine has had visions given by the Holy Spirit of being taken up to Heaven. There in Heaven, he has met Bach, Beethoven, Handel, and other great composers. Of course, most of the great musicians, scientists, and doctors of history past were devoted Christians. My friend shared with me how during his heavenly visions he would receive tips, suggestions, and instruction from these saints to help complete the music he has written. I have heard previews of this music and it causes one to get "goose bumps" upon hearing it. While my friend does have a mantle to create beautiful classical music that glorifies God, he still has to spend hours in his private studio to put it all together. Even with an anointing, there is a lot of work involved. He is very faithful to work hard to see God's Kingdom expanded through the field of musical arts that he is called to.

Make the most of a mantle by putting your whole heart into what God has called you to do. Determine to be the best in your specific field. Dismiss any thoughts of failure and why you can't succeed. Work hard and expect good things to happen to you.

Go far above and beyond the normal call of duty. As you do so, doors of increased anointing will open and you will be proven to be an invaluable asset to the Lord and to those around you.

## ENDNOTES

1. *Golden Grain* by John Wright Follette is public domain; *Golden Grain* and *Broken Bread* can both be viewed online at; Christian Classics Ethereal Library www.ccel.org.

2. Wikipedia: The Free Encyclopedia. Wikimedia Foundation Inc. Joan of Arc; accessed July 22, 2008.

.

CHAPTER 8

# Guidelines for Receiving a Mantle

Did you know that what you listen to the most is what will have the greatest influence in your life? We are told in the Bible to follow the faith of those who have taught us the Word of God.

> *Remember your leaders who spoke the word of God to you. Consider the outcome of their way of life and imitate their faith. Jesus Christ is the same yesterday and today and forever* (Hebrews 13:7-8 NIV).

Here in the Scriptures we are directed to remember the leaders in the church who taught us the Word of God. That's why I like reading the sermons of John G. Lake, Smith Wigglesworth, Kenneth Hagin, and others who build up my faith.

We are admonished to imitate their faith. The Word of God will produce results in our lives just as it produced results for them. We are to consider the outcome of their way of life. I've greatly considered the mystic saints and I've read their writings as well. Their writings bless me and inspire me to continually draw nearer to the Lord.

Mystics such as A. W. Tozer, Walter Beuttler, John Wright Follette, and many of the Catholic saints demonstrated living with a deep, passionate walk with the Lord. When these people left this planet to receive their heavenly reward, they graduated with honors. They did not have to sit in on all the A,B,C classes that many of God's children will have to attend upon arrival in Heaven. Many Christians fail to understand that if you don't learn basic Bible subjects down here you will have to learn them up there. I don't know about you, but when I get to Heaven, I don't want to sit in some elementary class about basic Christian doctrines that I was supposed to learn on the earth but never did. We should make great efforts during our earthly life to become as Christlike as possible. Once we cross over, our eternal rank is set.

*Whether a tree falls to the south or to the north, **in the place where it falls, there will it lie*** (Ecclesiastes 11:3 NIV).

Trees often symbolically speak of people. We determine what our heavenly rank will be by the way we live our lives on the earth. Once we die, that setting is established. There are many different levels in Heaven. We are not all lumped together in the same spiritual strata. Just like some stars shine with varying degrees of brightness, so it will be for the saints.

*Those who are wise will **shine like the brightness of the heavens,** and those who lead many to righteousness, **like the stars for ever and ever*** (Daniel 12:3 NIV).

There are faithful ministers that the Lord has used in my life and they have made a great impact for good in me. Over the years, my wife and I have supported solid ministries that teach and preach the Word of God. For us, it is an honor to financially support the quality ministries that the Lord has connected us with. As we are faithful to do this, we find that our ministry increases more and more in finances and scope of outreach.

## WHO WILL YOU LISTEN TO?

You must learn to be careful about whom you listen to and whom you follow spiritually. The reason this is so important is because you will in some measure become just like those you listen to.

When I was younger in the ministry I became aware of the prophetic calling upon my life. At that time, the Lord placed within my heart a desire to study the lives of ministers who operated in the ministry office of prophet. My study time found me examining the lives of many great ministers who are alive today and others who have gone on to be with the Lord. During my study, there was one particular man who stood out to me whose ministry greatly intrigued me. I enjoyed reading about his life and discovering the great miracles that took place in his meetings. In my heart, I wanted to be anointed to minister like this prophet did who has now gone on to be with the

Lord in Heaven. After reading many accounts of his life and ministry I decided to study his teachings. This is when things got interesting. Every time I tried to study his taped messages, the tape player would always mess up and stop working. The computer would never work right when I tried to download his audio messages from the Internet.

There were nights I stayed up late just trying to access old audio files of his taped messages that he preached while still alive, yet nothing ever worked. It was so frustrating until the Lord spoke to me and explained the situation. He told me His angels were *blocking me* from listening to this man's teaching because so much of his teaching during the latter part of his ministry was in error. How I thank God for His protection, which He so often provides through angels.

See, you have to be careful about who you follow because you will receive what another person has through contact and prolonged association. What you get around the most will eventually rub off on you. Of course, we want this principle to work for good and not for bad. Today I see many young people who I wish had a better understanding of this. They run with the wrong crowd and are swayed in their behavior by the influence of the larger group.

> *Do not be misled; "**Bad company corrupts good character.**" Come back to your senses as you ought, and stop sinning; for there are some who are ignorant of God—I say this to your shame* (1 Corinthians 15:33-34 NIV).

We should strive to live lives of holiness that glorify the Lord. We should stay away from things that have the appearance of evil. We should consider how others view our actions, particularly believers who are young in the Lord and also the unsaved. If you drink beer and participate in social drinking, people will automatically think you are a "party person." Even if you don't get drunk, you will still be viewed by those unsaved as a "partier" because that's what they do. If they see you drinking, they will automatically attach that label to you, because the advertising media has *taught* us that drinking beer in America is primarily associated with immoral sex. Don't throw the book at me! I'm just being honest. Look at the beer commercials. The commercials are totally lust-related. Anyone who would deny this has been without television for the last 30 years. We must consider others before ourselves. That's what love really is. The love of God makes you never want to offend or misguide someone. Even if your intentions are sincere, you will find that people will relate you to the present culture that surrounds you.

It has been many years now, but I remember when I used to drink beer. I was actually introduced to alcoholic beverages when I first started attending a Charismatic church! The pastor and all the elders loved their beer and wine and they always invited me to drink with them. Eventually, I agreed to do so. I immediately loved the taste of beer. There were certain brands that were my favorites.

I would justify my drinking by reminding myself that Paul told Timothy to drink a little wine because of his stomach problem. Well, I had no stomach problem, but I drank anyhow! Then, as I would drink my beer, I would remind myself that Jesus turned water into wine as His first miracle. Of course, I had no idea that the wines spoken of in the Bible were completely different than the wines that are available today. Bible wine was greatly diluted. You could get drunk off of it, but it would take hours to do so and you would have to drink several gallons of it in the process. Usually the water to wine dilution was at a rate of 20 to 1. These are widely known historical facts if one will only study them out.[1]

Over the years in my personal study tine I have spent many hours researching the subject of Bible wines. The wine Jesus drank was nothing like the wine you find available on supermarket shelves today. *Wine* in the Bible is a generic term. A comparably used term is *vehicle* which can also have several meanings, such as car, truck, van, SUV, etc. If you told people you drove a vehicle, they would wonder what kind of vehicle you were referring to. There are different types of wine mentioned in the Bible. A person needs to understand in context what type of wine is being spoken of upon its mention in the Bible. The primary method of preserving grape juice in the time of the Lord's earthly ministry was through boiling. The juice of the grape would be boiled immediately upon having been expressed from the grape. The remaining residue after boiling was known as *dibbs*. Dibbs was a thick, honey like syrup that would be placed in a wine-skin. When the sweet juice of the grape is boiled down to this consistency, it is impossible for it to ferment. It was much like what we know as orange juice concentrate. It could be reconstituted once water was added back to it. But when water was added back to reconstitute it for drinking purposes it was done so at a greatly diluted rate.

Let's suppose you could travel back through time and visit the twelve apostles during the Lord's earthly ministry. Before you travel back in time, you drop by your local grocery store and purchase a *modern-day* bottle of wine to take with you. If you went back in time and served that to the apostles, they would spit it out on the ground and be highly insulted. That is because in their day and time, it was common knowledge that only the pagans drank that *type* of wine. Those who drank **intoxicating wine** were considered by the Jews and early Christians to be "barbarians." If a person is willing to study the truth about the wines of the Bible and learn the laws of fermentation, then it will forever settle questions surrounding such topics as the miracle Jesus performed at the wedding in Cana of turning water into wine; Paul's permission to Timothy to use *a little wine*; the Lord's Supper at Corinth; and every other alcohol related question that some of God's people are not adequately prepared to answer.

These are things I was never taught in Charismatic Christianity. But when you study it out, you will find the truth, historical and factual evidence, plus good common sense to produce an overwhelming verdict to abstain from drinking alcohol.

# THE NEW WINE

For many years I have been a student of church history. I've studied countless revivals that have taken place in America and around the world. One consistent thing I've noticed amongst many observations is that when a full-blown move of God's Spirit comes to a town or a city, the liquor stores are the first businesses to be impacted. The bars, saloons, and liquor stores lose their customers. You would think if drinking alcohol were endorsed by God then logically the liquor business would flourish during revival. But when there is a genuine move of God's Spirit, the exact opposite takes place—the drinking establishments empty out because their customers have now gotten a taste of the new wine of the Holy Spirit and nothing else compares. There are also no detrimental effects of consuming large amounts of the new wine of the Holy Spirit.

After a period of time, the Lord began to deal with me about my beer drinking. Along with destroying my brain cells (I need all the ones I've got!) it gave a wrong appearance. So I made a firm commitment one night in prayer that I would no longer drink beer. I didn't have to make a commitment about wine because I've never liked the taste of alcoholic wine. As I made my commitment, I knew it was a settled issue.

The next day I was walking back from a bicycle shop where I had been looking at getting a new mountain bike. As I was walking home on the sidewalk, I was sweating profusely in the scorching heat, beneath a mid-day sun in the middle of summer in West Texas. It was hot—real hot—and I still had about two miles of walking before I would get home. Suddenly, I noticed a pickup truck pull up next to me and the driver rolled down his window. He slowly drove next to me and spoke through the window, saying, "Whew! It sure is a hot one today, isn't it?" I said, "Yeah, that sun's really beating down on me." He said, "You sure look thirsty, I've got something for ya' to cool you off." Having said that, he reached down and opened up a medium sized cooler that he had sitting in the front seat next to him. The cooler appeared to be packed with ice but he pushed his hand down into the bottom of it and pulled out a very cold can of beer. He said, "Here man, have a cold one on me!" For a few seconds I was shocked. Never before had anyone ever offered me free beer, much less when I was hot and thirsty. I said, "No thanks, I don't drink, but I appreciate the offer." He said, "Okay," and he drove off on down the road. The devil will test you to see if you mean business with God.

You have to ask yourself the question, "Is my drinking really necessary?" Aren't there hundreds of other options of beverages to choose from besides those containing alcohol? The government of love should determine everything we do in life. We are new creatures in Christ Jesus; we no longer live for ourselves. What would you think of me if after a meeting you saw me go out behind the back of the church and drink down a tall glass bottle of beer? What if you saw me in the pastor's office smoking a big cigar before I was to go out and minister to the people? Wouldn't that send up a big red flag for you questioning my character? It sure would for me if I saw those who consider themselves to be a men or women of God doing that. You would think, "If those people do that in public, what must they do in private?" There's enough opposition as it already is without going out and doing things that deliberately stir up problems. Others are watching you. Can you say with a clear conscience what Paul told the church in Corinth?

*Therefore I urge you to imitate me* (1 Corinthians 4:16 NIV).

Even as I was writing this very chapter, I received an unexpected knock on the door at midnight. This took place just as I finished writing the above verse mentioned by Paul. The "divine interruption" lasted a little over an hour, but now that it has been taken care of I can continue speaking with you. I believe the Lord wants me to share what just took place so you will expect the unexpected and be prepared.

Having heard the knock on the door, I went to answer it and found two young men standing outside, cold and slightly shaken up. They told me they had just lost control of their truck and crashed over the side of the road down a steep embankment. I went to the back window of the house and far down below I could see their truck off the road and in a very precarious situation where it looked like at any moment it could slip all the way down to the bottom of the ridge. The truck had gotten stuck on an old stump which prevented it from barreling down a ridge that had a steep vertical drop of several hundred feet. They were not hurt and were blessed to have gotten out of that mess without any injuries, especially since they were not wearing any seatbelts. We called the highway patrol, but because the house in which I am writing is way back in the rural mountains of North

Carolina, I knew it would be almost 30 minutes before they would arrive.

Because at this time it is winter with sub-freezing weather, I put them in my truck and drove down to the accident site and sat there in the truck with the heater blasting to keep us warm while we waited for the highway patrol. This gave me plenty of time to share the Gospel with them. Their ages were 18 and 20 and they belonged to a Baptist church, but they were not serving God. All I did for 30 minutes was minister to them the love and power of God. I explained to them how God's angels had protected them from serious injury. They listened to every word and were deeply thankful for my help.

When the highway patrol arrived, I had a good talk with the patrolman and then turned the young men over to his care as they then waited for the wrecker to pull the truck up from the ravine. Amazingly, the young men didn't have a scratch on them and their truck was totally fine except for a slight bend in the front bumper where it had caught on the stump. Before leaving, I was able to pray for those young men. The power of God touched their lives as they yielded their hearts to the Lord and were encouraged to serve the Lord with renewed passion. The Lord turned a potential deadly plan of the enemy into a divine appointment for blessing.

## OUR FREEDOM SHOULD NOT HINDER OTHERS

You have to be ready, because you never know when the Lord might call upon you to minister to somebody. What would have happened if I had been up late writing and drinking a six-pack of beer? Could I then effectively minister in a time of need? If I had been drinking, what would the highway patrol officer have thought of me as a minister of the Gospel with liquor on my breath? It's important to think about the bigger picture in life. It's not about any of us demanding our way or insisting upon our rights. I'm all for freedom, but our freedom should not hinder others or be a stumbling block to them.

The reverential fear of the Lord is going to come back into the Church. I'm not talking about legalism or a list of "you can't do this" and "you can't do that." We just need to live right and walk close with the Lord. The Holy Spirit will guide us into all truth. He will help us remove the slack from our lives and tighten up those areas that need special attention.

The things I'm talking about now are where the rubber meets the road. Reformation is coming to the Church. Fiery revivalists are going to begin appearing on the scene. You hardly hear any preaching in the church today against sin. Such topics are not popular, but change is coming. Revivalists walking in a Charles Finney, George Whitefield and Jonathan Edwards anointing will soon come on the scene. When they preach, their messages will not center around motivational topics such as, "God has Called You to be a Champion," or "Seven Steps to Success." Instead, their messages will carry the convicting power of the Holy Spirit. After these messages, you will not want to go to the church coffee shop and get a latté. You might just want to go lay down somewhere and try to assimilate the fire from Heaven.

Endeavor to live a life that is pleasing to the Lord, which uplifts your brothers and sisters in Christ. Be a good example at your work. Put forth 100 percent effort in all that you do so that the Lord is glorified. Mantles come to those who are qualified for the position, not to those who are just sitting around hoping something will happen.

It is important to remember that just because a person operates in the gifts of the Spirit does not mean that person's life is pleasing to the Lord. God's Word tells us in First Corinthians chapter 13 that we can do all kinds of wonderful things, but if we don't have love we are nothing. Make sure the person you follow walks in love and is genuine in service to the Lord. This one area of the love walk has got to be one of the biggest areas that the Church must improve in. Arrogance, elitism, pride, bickering, quarrelling, and backbiting are running rampant in Charismatic circles. These insecurities and carnal expressions must be replaced with the pure love of Christ. We must overcome evil with good.

Many years back when I was just newly filled with the Holy Spirit, I experienced something that helped me better plan for my future. For months I would listen to a prophet who was a well-known minister on the radio. I loved his preaching. He was electric in his personality and had tremendous gifts of the Spirit take place in his meetings. When he came to my hometown to hold meetings in a local church, I even rode my bicycle twelve miles each way to see him minister. (I didn't have a car at that time.) To me he was the greatest minister I had ever seen. In my heart I so wanted to be like him.

One day as I was on my way to work, I stopped by the doughnut shop to get a doughnut. This wasn't a normal habit of mine because at that time in my life I rarely had the extra money to buy a doughnut and coffee. But sometimes you still have to treat yourself, so I went inside the doughnut shop and got in line and then, to my shock, I noticed standing right in front of me in the line was the famous prophet! I was overcome with joy, but I managed to act normal and I said "Hello" to him. I told him how much I appreciated his radio program. He thanked me and then turned back around. He ordered his doughnut and went and took a seat. I ordered my doughnut and went to find a seat but they were all taken. This minister was sitting by himself and I thought to myself, "This is the chance of a lifetime." I summoned my courage and I went over and nicely asked him if I could sit at the table with him.

He slowly responded, "Well, I guess." He didn't seem too excited about his new guest, so he picked up his newspaper and began to silently read. I tried to ask him a few questions about the things of God, but he seemed completely disinterested in me. He would give me a one word answer and go right back to reading his newspaper. After about ten minutes he got up to leave. His final words were, "It was nice meeting you. Good-bye." Those two sentences alone consisted of 95 percent of our conversation at the table. Basically, he didn't give me the time of day. I can't say I was devastated by this, because by this point in my life I had already grown numb to such treatment from religious leaders. It seemed the only ones the church leaders took interest in were the ones with deep pockets. However, that conversation, or lack of one, instilled something in me that is a core principle of my life.

Love is the greatest thing. James said in his epistle that if you put a rich man on the front row and at the same time make the poor man stand up in the back of the church, then you have committed sin. I like James. He let it rip and he could not be controlled by the big givers in the church. He was controlled by the Word. Since that day at the doughnut shop, I've always tried to be a person who, through the love of God, can connect with anyone, regardless of that person's condition. Whether they are rich or poor, black or white, or of any other background, I want to be a person who cares about others. Paul said:

> *Be of the same mind toward one another; do not be haughty in mind, but associate with the lowly* (Romans 12:16 NASB).

My wife and I try to connect and work with fellow ministries that exhibit strong characteristics of the love of Christ. We might not all agree eye to eye on every issue, but that's not the point. We might make mistakes because none of us are perfect. But I tell you right now I connect with those who major on the majors. And love will always be a major connecting point. Walk in love. Take the road less traveled. In the end you will walk in the mantle destined for you and your calling will be fulfilled.

## ENDNOTE

1. *Snake in the Glass* by Dr. Bruno Caporrimo. This book gives a detailed view of Old and New Testament wines. It describes the history, production process, and

chemical composition of what Bible wines actually were. The author spent eleven years studying Bible wines and did his doctoral dissertation on this subject. Website: www.echipministry.com.

# CHAPTER 9

# *Let the Holy Spirit Choose Your Mantle*

Ask the Lord and trust Him to reveal to you the mantle that He has planned for you to receive. Don't try to figure out with your natural mind what mantle God has in store for you. You can't figure out spiritual things with natural thinking. Allow the Holy Spirit to lead you through the inward witness in the direction He has for you to go. Some people think you can go out and choose a mantle much like you would choose food at a grocery store. It doesn't work that way. However, choosing a mantle is much like choosing a spouse.

When I was single and wanting to get married, I let the Lord pick my wife for me and I sure got blessed. Not only is my wife beautiful, but we are best friends as well. Our marriage was made in Heaven and I received God's best for my life. It sure pays to let God reveal to you His best choice. Of course, it takes setting aside time in prayer to get a clear leading of the Holy Spirit concerning God's perfect will in matters, but it is time well spent.

You may think that right now you know the mantle you want to receive, but be patient and give the Holy Spirit time to lead you concerning this. Most young ministers naturally think they want the mantle of the famous television evangelist because that person is popular and well known, but you can't choose that way. Actually, the Lord will not give a mantle for ministry to someone who is not called into the ministry. There are five ministry offices spoken of in Ephesians chapter 4. They are the apostle, prophet, evangelist, pastor, and teacher (see Eph. 4:11). There is also the ministry of helps, which covers a vast area of Christian service, but this is different from a calling to the five-fold ministry.

We also see in Scripture the mention of the ministry of reconciliation. But every believer is called to this ministry, which is to reconcile the lost back to God. Don't let this discourage you if you want to draw nearer to the Lord. You don't have to be in the ministry to be spiritual! You don't have to stand in a ministry office and preach behind a pulpit to be someone who has a close walk with God. I've met housewives, plumbers, businessmen, businesswomen, and a host of other good people working stable and regular jobs who spiritually speaking would run circles around some ministers. Not being called into the ministry is not a handicap in your knowing God. God is no respecter of persons (see Acts 10:34). He will reveal Himself in incremental levels to anyone who seeks His face.

Elisha asked Elijah for a double portion as we saw earlier in our study. Elisha was actually asking for a double portion to stand in the same ministry office that Elijah stood in, which was that of the prophet. Elisha could ask for this because God called him into the ministry office of the prophet.

It would be a waste of time for me to ask God for a double portion of the anointing that was upon Albert Einstein's life to be upon mine. Why? Because I am not called into the career field of scientific and mathematical studies. If my old high school Algebra teacher were reading this, I'm sure she would give a hearty "Amen!" You have to find your gifting and calling in life and develop that to its fullest potential. There are countless mantles available not only for ministry, but also for every occupation imaginable. Someone might say, "That's great, but which one is best?" The mantle that is best and the career that is best is the one that God has chosen for you! Don't be concerned about what others may be doing, but joyfully accept whatever assignment God has for you. That is where your joy will be and that is also where you will prosper.

## BE OPEN

A person should be open to God's plan. We are in a time and season where valuable mantles that have been captured and placed in the enemy's camp are being taken back. You may be surprised at what God wants to give to you. The New Age has stolen much of what belongs to the Church. Much has been lost through default because the Church stepped back from the supernatural and let the New Age take it. Even the term *New Age* belongs to the Church, for when Jesus rules for a thousand years upon the earth we will have entered a "new age."

Once in a meeting I taught a message from Psalm 92 about how we need to be anointed with fresh oil. I read from the old King James Version because I like the way it translates that verse.

> *But My horn shalt thou exalt **like the horn of a unicorn:** I shall be anointed with fresh oil* (Psalm 92:10 KJV).

After the meeting a woman came up to me with a look on her face of fear and concern. With great trepidation she said, "Brother Steven, aren't unicorns associated with the New Age? Isn't that of the devil?" I couldn't help but grin at her statement. Some people have developed such paranoia of the devil. In a reverse form, they almost reverence him—they give the enemy way too much respect. I spoke with her for awhile and tried to get her focus away from associating anything supernatural or mystical with being of the devil. Some people see a demon behind every rock. I prefer to believe there's an angel behind those rocks. Others see the devil running around causing havoc everywhere. I see God everywhere, reaching out to reveal Himself to all who genuinely seek for Him.

> *God did this so that men would seek Him and perhaps reach out for Him and find Him, **though He is not far from each one of us*** (Acts 17:27 NIV).

152

The enemy has lied to the Church just like he lied to Eve. The devil has attempted to put fear in the Church regarding anything that is supernatural. Some Christians are even afraid of the rainbow. They associate the rainbow as being a symbol of the New Age. But the rainbow encircles the throne of God. The rainbow was in Heaven first and belongs to God and His people. Once I was taken up in the spirit realm where I saw the Pegasus horse. It is a flying horse that has wings. These things belong to God; they are His property.

## Marco Polo's Journey to China

Mantles to walk in the Spirit are falling upon the people of God. On the cross, Jesus purchased for us a full inheritance that includes the supernatural manifestations of His Spirit. God is beginning to move His people further out in the realm of the Spirit to explore the vast wonders of His glory. It is similar in many ways to what Marco Polo experienced during his journey to China.

In the year 1271 a young man at the age of seventeen left his home in Venice, Italy, to travel with his father and uncle to China. Marco Polo was very familiar with having seen the best and finest that the Mediterranean region had to offer, because he was raised in a wealthy family. He knew the Bible well and understood the theology of the Latin Church. However, there was another country far away of which the Europeans had only heard unconfirmed rumors. Marco Polo would become the first Westerner to bring back a full, detailed report of what he saw during his travels throughout China.

After a journey of three and a half years that covered a distance of 5,600 miles, they arrived in China at Shang-tu which was the summer palace of the Emperor Kublai Khan. They were personally greeted by the Emperor, and young Marco found great favor with the Khan.

Because Marco was a gifted linguist and fluent in four languages, he was offered an official position in the king's court. He was assigned as an emissary and was sent on special missions by the Emperor. Marco was amazed at the Emperor's winter palace in Beijing, which eventually became the capital city. He described it as being, "the greatest palace that ever was."

The walls of the palace were covered with gold and silver, and the hall area of the palace could seat over 6000 people for special dining events. It was also at the Beijing palace where Emperor Khan kept a stud of 10,000 horses that were completely white without any spot. The horse's milk was allocated for the emperor's family and for any tribe that had won a victory in battle for the former Emperor Genghis Khan. Kublai Khan also had seeds of steppe grass sown in the courtyard of the Imperial Palace because it reminded him of his family roots in Mongolia.

Marco traveled extensively throughout China on assignments by the Emperor. He was awed by the great military power and the financial wealth that the nation possessed.

China's huge empire easily dwarfed that of Europe. But his favorite city in China was Hangchow. Upon Marco's arrival in Hangchow, he was amazed at what he saw. There were landscaped highways, public parks, boat marinas, and vast numbers of arched canals. Many of the arches were tall enough for large ships with high masts to pass beneath. There was an advanced underground septic and sewer system that serviced the entire city. Policemen were in abundance and there also was in operation a highly developed fire brigade.

Even the postal system was outstanding. There were three levels of expedited mail delivery. There was *second class, first class,* and *Top Priority—On His Imperial Majesty's Service. Second class* mail was carried by foot runners who had stations every three miles. They would switch runners at each station. This system allowed a normal ten-day message to arrive within 24 hours. *First class* mail was transported on horseback with relay stages every 25 miles. But the *Top Priority* mail that was sent by the Emperor was transported by non-stop horsemen who carried a special tablet that was inscribed with the sign of the gerfalcon. At each relay station a fresh horse would be brought out for the courier with the Top Priority mail.

Marco said this system allowed the horsemen to carry a message to its destination of over 300 miles away in one day. In Hangchow, you could purchase paperback books, eat gourmet meals in fine porcelain bowls, wear garments of pure silk, and live in a level of prosperity that no city in Europe could touch.

Marco, along with his father and uncle, stayed in the Khan's court for 17 years. During this time they acquired great wealth and riches. As the Khan grew older into his seventies, they decided to leave China or else they could possibly encounter a difficult time getting their wealth out of the country upon the

Khan's eventual death. With the Khan's blessing, they left and after several years of enduring the long journey home, they finally arrived back in Venice, Italy. They had been gone for 24 years!

Upon their arrival, no one recognized them. Even their own servants refused them entrance into their former villa. The Polos had long been given up for dead. However, because of the wealth they returned with, they eventually convinced some. Three years after his return to Venice, Marco commanded a galley in a war against the rival city of Genoa. He was captured during the fighting and spent a year in prison. This worked out remarkably well, because there was another man in prison who happened to be a gifted writer. At this man's prompting, Marco dictated the full story of his travels. After one year in prison, the men were released and Marco's story was made into a book. The book immediately made a tremendous impact within contemporary Europe. It was titled *The Description of the World*, but it quickly became known as "Il Milione" (The Million Lies).

Countless people read the book, but many questioned Marco's stories. Such stories seemed outlandish and far-fetched. His mention of "nuts the size of a man's head, full of milk" (coconuts), and "cloth that can not be consumed by fire" (asbestos) and "vast wealth where coins are not used as money" (paper currency) were just too much for many Europeans to accept as truth. Marco went on to marry, have children, and lived to the age of 70. Upon his deathbed in 1324, just before he died, a priest urged him to retract some of his tallest tales. With his last breath, he confidently said, "I have not told half of what I saw!"[1]

We must go on with God. You don't need to wait for your best friend, spouse, or a family member to make the move. You make the decision to move on with God. God's moving and He's waiting for many of His people to catch up. There are many experiences the Lord has allowed me to have in the Holy Spirit. Many times I'm reluctant to tell such stories because some Christians do not have enough of the Word in them to help them understand spiritual principles. In some meetings I simply teach the basics, because I know it would do more harm than good to try and talk about the deeper spiritual life if the people are not ready. Paul told the Hebrew Christians they were not prepared for mature teaching. They were still at an infant stage of spiritual development, even though they had been believers for quite some time.

> *In fact, though by this time you ought to be teachers, you need someone to teach you the elementary truths of God's word all over again. You need milk, not solid food!* (Hebrews 5:12 NIV)

But there are still valid, genuine experiences that do take place by the Spirit of God. By the grace of God I have met the Lord Jesus Christ several times in person. I've spoken with angels and have asked them questions. The Lord has even allowed me to meet some of the redeemed saints during my times of being caught up in the Spirit. On one occasion I met William Seymour who was one of the men the Lord used during the Azusa Street Revival of 1906. During this vision William Seymour encouraged me to pray especially for children who suffer from sickness, disease, and physical and emotional abuse. As I have stepped out in faith to do this, we have seen the Lord greatly touch the children. I'm certainly not the only one these experiences are happening to. But for the most part I have discovered that the realm of the Spirit is a vast realm of spiritual reality that lays largely unexplored. We need more spiritual Marco Polos who are willing to make the sacrifices to see what lies beyond our present knowledge.

The same is true in the natural realm. The earth is crying out for the sons of God to be revealed (see Rom. 8:19). The natural creation longs to be free from the elements of sin. This is why Sadhu Sundar Singh had such remarkable experiences with wild animals during his apostolic journeys. His deep walk with God affected the natural creation around him. A panther, leopard, and cobra are just a few of the animals he met and dealt successfully with on his trips through remote areas. His experiences read like something out of a fairy-tale; yet they were real, and some were seen by witnesses. I would like to share with you just one of the many encounters this man had with the animal kingdom.

I have always loved reading and I'm a collector of hard-to-find books. Once I ministered in a church of a dear pastor friend of mine in Central California. After the meetings were over, he gave me a very precious gift. It was an old book in excellent condition that was printed in 1934 about the life of Sadhu Sundar Singh. The book was written by a close, personal friend of the Sadhu. (The word *Sadhu* in India means *Teacher*.) The author of this book (C.F. Andrews) shares the story of an Indian man (Shoran Singha) who was a personal eyewitness of an uncanny event that happened to the Sadhu.

> One night just before we went to bed, we noticed lights moving in the valley, and the Sadhu explained to me that men were probably in pursuit of a leopard…Long after midnight I was aroused by a movement in the room. The Sadhu had risen from his bed and was moving towards the door, which opened on the wooden stairs outside the house. The creaking of the wood made it clear that he was going down. Knowing that the Sadhu spent hours of the night in prayer, I was not surprised at this. But when half an hour or so had passed and he had not returned, I became uneasy; the thought of the leopard in the valley made me feel anxious.

> So I got out of bed, passed into the dressing room, and looked out of the window toward the forest. A few yards from the house I saw the Sadhu sitting, looking down into the deep valley. It was a beautiful night. The stars were shining brightly; a light wind rustled the leaves of the trees. For a few moments I watched the silent figure of the Sadhu. Then my eyes were attracted by something moving on his right. An animal was coming towards him. As it got nearer, I saw that it was a leopard. Choked with fear, I stood motionless near the window, unable even to call. Just then, the Sadhu turned his face towards the animal and held out his hand. As though it had been a dog, the leopard lay down and stretched out its head to be stroked.

It was a strange, unbelievable scene, and I can never forget it. A short time afterwards the Sadhu returned and was soon asleep, but I lay awake wondering what gave that man such power over wild animals.

After the author shared in his book the personal testimony of Shoran Singha, he then added his own comments, stating:

This is Shoran Signha's story of what he actually saw that night. When I questioned him closely about it, he told me how he was so benumbed by fear that he could not even cry out. It all happened at a place in Bareri, which I know so well that I can still easily re-call every detail to mind. Therefore, I have confidence that the incident occurred as Shoran has described it. He goes on to relate how in the morning he had asked the Sadhu, "Were you not frightened when you saw the leopard?" "Why should the leopard harm me?" he replied. "I was not his enemy. Moreover, as long as I trust in Christ, I have no cause to tremble."

On another occasion, however, the Sadhu himself tells us that he was terrified. He woke up in a cave, where he had spent the night, and found a large leopard be-side him. He confessed afterwards that for a moment he was almost paralyzed with fear; for he was taken quite unawares. But, once outside the cave, his courage returned, and he gave thanks to God who had thus preserved his life.[2]

Let the Holy Spirit choose your mantle. God has something special for you. Open your heart to the new and fresh anointing that God wants you to receive. Let the wonders of the spiritual and natural world become a greater reality in your life. God wants to give you His very best!

## ENDNOTES

1. www.brainyquote.com.

2. *Sadhu Sundar Singh* by C.F. Andrews is public domain; Hodder & Stoughton Limited London—1934; pages 164-168.

# CHAPTER 10

# *How I Received My First Mantle*

We have examined scriptural examples of how mantles are transferred and how the anointing can be imparted from one individual to another. We have also observed the lives of certain saints in recent church history who have had mantles transferred to them through serving, close association, dreams, visions, or angelic visitations. Through the years, I have received various mantles as I have progressed in my walk with the Lord. Now I would like to share with you how I received my first mantle from the Lord.

At times, the Lord will speak to me through dreams at night while I am asleep. These are not simple little dreams that you can vaguely remember when you wake up, but rather the type of dreams that have a weight to them and are crystal clear and straightforward in understanding. Dreams are also referred to in the Bible as *night visions*. It was through a night vision that the Lord chose to impart a mantle to me.

> *Then the secret was revealed to Daniel in a **night vision**. So Daniel blessed the God of heaven* (Daniel 2:19).

> *At Gibeon the LORD appeared to Solomon during the **night in a dream**, and God said, "Ask for whatever you want me to give you"* (1 Kings 3:5 NIV).

We see clearly with Solomon that his dream was a real encounter with the Lord. The Lord did not appear to him while he was awake, but waited until he was asleep. The bottom line is that whether it happened to be a dream or a wide-awake experience, we see that the purpose was still accomplished—Solomon received what he asked for.

I must admit that when I went to bed that night I had no idea an experience like this was going to take place. That night, I actually went to bed somewhat discouraged. For a little over two years I had sought the Lord for a mantle but nothing ever happened. In my times of prayer I would talk with the Lord about how Elijah transferred the mantle to Elisha. Within my heart I sensed the Lord had a mantle for me, but after two years of praying I still had not received one. As I lay down in bed that night I was discouraged but I still knew God would answer my prayer in His timing. I quickly fell off into a deep sleep and began to have a dream.

In this dream I was transported into the realm of the second heaven. Have you ever been out on a beautiful day when there were no clouds in the sky and looked up to see a jet flying high overhead? It was in this realm about six or seven miles straight up where the Lord took me, but I was carried there in the spirit realm. The first heaven is the realm we live in on earth. The second heaven above us is the realm where satan has his kingdom of darkness established. From this position of the earth's upper atmosphere, he plans and launches his evil attacks upon humankind. He rules over the lives of those in spiritual darkness as the prince of the power of the air. The demons and evil spirits on the earth get their orders from the headquarters of darkness that circles the earth in the second heaven. Angels from Heaven have to break through this realm to reach us here on earth. At times, angels can travel with little or no resistance by moving through portals that reach from Heaven to earth. Other times, they are sent by God into areas that do not have an established portal. When this is the case, they may encounter the resistance of enemy forces found in the second heaven. We see this spiritual parallel in the following verse concerning how a heavenly messenger broke through demonic resistance to reach Daniel.

> *But the prince of the Persian kingdom resisted me twenty-one days. Then Michael, one of the chief princes, came to help me because I was detained there with the king of Persia* (Daniel 10:13 NIV).

> *So he said, "Do you know why I have come to you? Soon I will return to fight against the prince of Persia, and when I go,*

*the prince of Greece will come; but first I will tell you what is written in the Book of Truth. (No one supports me against them except Michael, your prince.)* (Daniel 10:20-21 NIV)

There are great spiritual battles that are fought in the second heaven. That is why it is so important for us to pray and be persistent in our prayers. Although Jesus has completely defeated satan and all the powers of darkness through His death, burial, and triumphant resurrection, we must enforce the devil's defeat. If we do not pray and exercise our God-given authority as believers in Christ, then the enemy will try to delay, hinder, or prevent the will of God from occurring. The third Heaven is the heavenly realm of Paradise. In this realm, no evil can enter.

*I know a man in Christ who fourteen years ago was caught up to the **third heaven**. Whether it was in the body or out of the body I do not know—God knows. And I know that this man—whether in the body or apart from the body I do not know, but God knows—was **caught up to paradise** (2 Corinthians 12:2-4a NIV).*

Now, back to the night vision I was sharing. As I reached my destination in the second heaven I arrived behind a large outcropping of rocks. As I peered over the rocks, I could see down into a valley where there appeared to be an enemy camp. In this camp I noticed fierce looking demons marching around something that they were trying to protect. These large demons had huge razor sharp spears that looked to be about eighteen feet long. Some of the demons were well over ten feet tall. Over the top of the enemy camp flew two huge evil spirits that were completely black, having the appearance of bats. They had large, leathery looking wings with knife-like talons and claws on their feet and at the tips of their wings. Their sharp beaks were polished black like oversized crows. As I watched this bizarre sight, the thought formed in my mind that I sure would like to get down to that camp and see what they were guarding.

No sooner had that thought formed in my mind when suddenly, over my left shoulder, flew two huge white angels with wings! These big angels flew down into the enemy camp with incredible speed and quickly circled the camp several times. These two angels were so fast that they flew in between the demonic bat creatures with rapid, darting moves. In one way, the two angels reminded me of an aerial exhibition I saw a few years earlier by the Navy's Blue Angels elite flight team. Their movements were powerful, precise, and daring. This only served to stir up the demons into a wild frenzy while the two white angels took off in blazing speed. The demons were so enraged by this provocative act that the entire enemy camp, including the flying bat creatures, took off in pursuit of the two angels. The entire camp was now left completely unguarded!

It was then I heard the voice of the Lord speak to me, saying, "Go quickly, those are My decoy angels." I ran down that hill into the valley as fast as I could and to my surprise I ran up to a large stack of clothing! In this stack of clothing I saw hats, gloves, shirts, coats, scarves, boots, shoes, and many other kinds of clothing. The density of the pile was enormous compared to the actual size of the pile, which was about five feet high and shaped like a rectangle. The stack of clothing was only about ten feet long and five feet wide. But within this small pile were thousands upon thousands of pieces of clothing. I said, "Lord, what is all of this clothing?" He said, "These are unclaimed mantles." He continued by saying, "My people from times past have come home to be with Me in Heaven, but when they left this world no one ever claimed their mantles. They are waiting to be claimed."

Without a moment's hesitation I somehow knew exactly which mantle was for me. I reached deeply into the center of the pile with my right arm. I reached so far into the pile that the clothes in the stack actually touched my shoulder. Grabbing hold of my mantle I then pulled out, to my surprise, a beautiful blue sweatshirt! You have to understand that blue has always been my favorite color and sweatshirts are my favorite things to wear. I pulled it over my head and pushed my arms through the long sleeves. Ahhh, a perfect fit!

The voice of the Lord then came to me and told me exactly who it was that had previously worn the mantle. He said it belonged to one of His trusted prophets who lived his life out fully on the earth and was now in Heaven. The Lord even shared with me his name and where he used to live.

It was only about two weeks after this event took place that I actually found a book which recorded many of the events of this man's life. Although he lived hundreds of years ago, there were accurate writings made about many of the miracles that happened in this man's ministry. As I read through the book, I noticed very similar personality traits that he and I both have. I also like the fact that he lived to be of great age.

After this experience, I continued on with my ministry, but there was a noticeable change. People would come up to me after meetings and tell me how much I had progressed spiritually since they last saw me. It was also only a short time after receiving the first mantle that the supernatural realm began to open up to me like never before. Upon studying the life of the former prophet, I found he had a life marked with angelic visitations and heavenly experiences. I'm so glad I allowed the Lord to choose the right mantle for me. Although the Lord has now taken me on into the apostolic ministry, I still love moving in that prophetic anointing. Glory to God!

After receiving this dream from the Lord, I shared it with several respected ministry leaders. One of these leaders is a pastor of a church who has been through many trials and hardships, yet he is still moving forward in the work God has called him to do. Without him knowing about this dream, I called him up on the phone to greet him and to see how he was doing. As we shared in conversation, he on his own initiative said that God had told him 11 years ago that the mantle for the city where his church is located would be his if he persevered. Despite other churches in the same area coming and going, he is still laboring and trusting God to fulfill His word to him. When I shared the dream with him, he lit up on the other end of the phone like a light bulb. This wasn't planned, but when I was talking to him about the dream, I realized I was wearing a blue sweatshirt. The Lord then moved upon me strongly to minister to him prophetically and we were both blessed.

Shortly after this my wife and I were having dinner with a respected evangelist and his wife. After a great meal and fellowship, my wife suggested I share the recent experience about the dream regarding the mantles. Upon hearing the dream, the evangelist suddenly lost interest in his delicious tiramisu dessert. He wanted his mantle! That evening he left with a divine desire imparted within his heart to find the mantle God had prepared for him. Certainly for him it is some type of healing mantle, which will greatly enhance his ministry, thus bringing the Lord increased glory and honor.

The Lord has a mantle for you to receive. In these last days we are going to see mantles merge together to form new expressions of God's glory never seen in the earth before. You might be surprised at what mantle comes falling toward you from Heaven.

Once I went to minister in Nevada at a church that loves the moving of God's Spirit. I wasn't scheduled to minister until Sunday morning, but I arrived earlier in the week, on a Friday morning. The pastor shared with me that the church had a prayer meeting every Friday night and he invited me to come. I agreed to come along; no one has to twist my arm to go to a prayer meeting because I love to pray with the saints. Once there, the church began to pray and it was a great time of intercession for the city, state, and our nation. After over an hour of prayer, I went and sat down on the steps leading up to the pulpit and began to pray in the Spirit. While I was sitting there, I noticed mantles begin to fall through the roof of the church building. They would come toward certain people and hover over them. I thought to myself, "Lord, I'm not even going to say anything because this church knows I've done extensive teaching on the subject of mantles. If I say something they'll probably think I'm mantle crazy!" So I just sat there and watched mantles float through the air of that church's sanctuary.

Sunday morning rolled around and I was scheduled to minister in the morning service. That morning, as the pastor of the church walked into the building, everyone was surprised to see him wearing an expensive three-piece suit. This was far from his normal style of dress. Usually he would wear blue jeans and a nice shirt. On other occasions he might put on a sport-coat with his jeans if he felt like being dressier. But a three-piece suit for him was almost unheard of. The church wondered what was going on. As he stepped behind the pulpit that morning, he explained his reason for his step-up in clothing.

He said, "Friday night in the prayer meeting as we were praying, I heard a sound and I looked up and I saw a mantle coming toward me. It looked like a shawl that would go over your shoulders and it was completely black. Because of the black color, I resisted receiving it because I thought the color could perhaps represent sin. The Lord saw my hesitancy and so He spoke to me and said, "What color is gunpowder?" I said, "Lord, its black." He replied, "This is a mantle of **heavenly gunpowder**, I desire for you to receive it!" The pastor yielded his heart to receive and he said that black mantle descended and gently came to rest upon his shoulders.

The pastor then announced to the church, "Today Brother Steven is here with us and he and I are going to minister to the sick. I'm going to put this new mantle into action right now. If you are sick, come forward in faith and you will be healed by the power of God." As I stood there that day next to him, it was a joy to see that anointing of healing power flow out of his hands and go right into the diseased areas of people's bodies. The Lord opened my eyes to see it in the spirit realm. It looked like a pure, white liquid substance flowing out of his hands. There was some power present that day and notable miracles took place as he and I did a tag-team attack on sickness and disease.

The meeting that morning lasted much longer than normal because of the glorious time we were all having in the Lord. After it was over, the pastor and I both were physically tired. Along with our wives, we decided to go get something light to eat. We thought a coffee house would be good because we could all use a good coffee. We randomly picked a coffee house in an area of town that neither of us had gone to before. I ended up getting my coffee first, so I went and grabbed a table that was outside in a pretty atrium setting. I sat down in the chair and took a big drink of my coffee. It sure tasted good. It's nice to enjoy the fruit of your labors!

When I sat my drink down on the table I noticed for the first time strange writing all over the table. It appeared someone had taken a can of spray-paint and sprayed in big black letters all over the table the words "**Heavenly Gunpowder.**" At that moment Kelly and the other pastor and his wife arrived at the table. I told them to look at the table. When the pastor saw it he almost dropped his coffee. He said, "I wouldn't have believed that unless I saw it with my own eyes!" Kelly went back inside the coffee house to ask them what this meant. The worker at the counter said, "Oh, that's the name of a Chinese tea we sell here. It has a real kick!" We all rejoiced at this divine confirmation while we thanked God for His explosive healing power.

## YOUR UNIQUE MANTLE

God has a mantle that's unique for you. Prepare your heart to receive God's very best for your life. I've discovered that the Lord has a sense of humor. You can expect God to connect with you in a way that is unmistakably Him.

Once when I was ministering in Southern California I had a friend who is a ministry partner call me and suggest that I contact a Christian friend of hers who is an international businessman who was in town for a few days. My friend who lives in Los Angeles said to me, "I know you don't know this man, but I believe you are supposed to meet him." I said, "Okay, where is he staying?" "At the Beverly Hills Hilton," she replied. I got the businessman's telephone number from my friend and called him to set up an appointment just for him and me to fellowship and get to know one another. I drove over to the hotel and met him on a certain day for lunch.

During our lunch conversation we had a great talk as we both discussed certain issues that the Holy Spirit was emphasizing for the Church. During our talk, I felt certain the Holy Spirit would share with me a prophetic word for this man, but

I never could get anything to share. I've learned over the years that if you don't have anything from the Spirit of God then don't manufacture something in the flesh. The only leading I got from the Holy Spirit was to share with this man a small book I had written called, *"Where are the Mantles?"* This was the first book I had written and it was self-published. After our meal, I gave him a copy of my book which was actually a very short, abbreviated form of the up-to-date and greatly expanded book you are now holding in your hands. He thanked me for the book and for our time together and then we both went our separate ways.

Two days later I received a call from this man. He said the day he received my book he read it later that night while at the hotel. It only took him a little less then an hour to read all the way through it because it wasn't very long. After completing the book, he then prayed and sincerely asked God to give to him the mantle that was assigned for him.

He then shared with me how the next day he was supposed to have flown from Los Angeles to Switzerland for a business meeting but he decided to make a detour and stop at a certain church in Northern California to see some friends. While at this church he was told that there was a prophetess who happened to be there. His friends asked him if he would be open to allow this woman of God to minister to him prophetically. As a Spirit-filled believer he said, "Sure, I love prophecy. Let's see what she has to say." They took him to meet her, and when the prophetess saw the businessman she said, "Step forward!" As he stepped forward, she looked at him with spiritual vision and she said to him, "You've got the wrong mantle on, step backward." As he stepped back, the woman of God reached her hand behind him and made a cutting motion with her arm, appearing to be severing the hindering plans of the enemy that had frustrated this man's finances. Having done this she then said, "Step forward. You now have a new mantle. It is the mantle you have asked the Lord for. It is a mantle of gold."

Remember, when the Lord gives you a mantle—a special anointing—it will identify with who God made you to be. The Lord knows how to tie things together. The Lord gave this man a mantle of gold. What the prophetess did not know was that this man had just asked to receive his heavenly mantle, and she was also not aware that a primary facet of his business dealings involve investments in gold. Since that day, my businessman friend has continued to move forward in his particular calling of international investment with increased authority and anointing from the Lord. When God calls you to accomplish a certain task, He will also place upon you the mantle to get the job done.

# CHAPTER 11

# *Mantles Are Falling*

Several years back at a pastor's conference held in Southern California, the Lord had me minister from the Bible on the subject of mantles. After completing my teaching, the Holy Spirit moved upon my heart to minister prophetically to several individuals in the audience.

A young married couple had come forward who wanted to receive prayer. As soon as I saw them, my eyes were opened in the spirit realm and I could see from Heaven two mantles floating down and coming to rest across their shoulders. Keep in mind that I saw this in the Spirit through the gift of discerning of spirits. In the natural realm they were both wearing nice dress clothes that people normally wear to church. In the

Spirit, however, I saw them each having a beautiful cloth that was intricately embroidered with all types of flowers draped over their shoulders.

Out loud I said, "You are both called to preach the Gospel in Holland!" In the Holy Spirit, I knew the flowers represented Holland. They both fell backward and were gently lowered to the floor by the ushers standing behind them. The pastor of the church then walked up and I passed him the microphone, and he said, "Brother Steven does not know this, but in several months I will be leaving to go and preach the Gospel in Holland, and the Lord told me to take this young couple with me."

Mantles from Heaven are still falling today. I've seen it happen many times. When my wife and I moved from out West and across the country to Moravian Falls, North Carolina, we did not know anybody in the whole state of North Carolina. We simply moved there by faith based upon the leading of the Holy Spirit. It has now been a few years since that move and we now have many wonderful friendships that the Lord has established.

I remember one interesting event that took place when we were still brand new to the area. We had been out on the road ministering from state to state while traveling in our motor home. After having been on the road non-stop for over three months, we returned to Moravian Falls. At this time, we still had all of our belongings in a local storage facility and we would stay at a large guest lodge when we were in town. We stayed at this lodge for a short period of time while we were locating a place to live. When I pulled the motor home up to the lodge after such a long trip, I was physically tired from having driven all day long and also from having been on the road for such an extended period of time. It was about 5 P.M. when we arrived at the lodge.

As I stepped out of the motor home and stretched my legs, I was thanking the Lord for helping us complete another long ministry circuit of coast to coast travel with lots of ministry packed into it. While I was just walking around relaxing, I came across a friend who was going into the lodge. This woman was one of only four people whom my wife and I had met during our brief time in the town. We were still so new that we only knew four people! When she saw me, she said, "Hey, I'm hosting a minister's meeting tonight at the lodge. Why don't you and your wife come and join us?" I thanked her for the invitation and told her we would think about. To be honest, I didn't want to go because I was tired and also because the meeting was going to start in only forty-five minutes.

After driving all day, I sure didn't look my best. Driving over five hundred miles every day had made my head feel like I was still moving, even though I was standing on solid ground. It's kind of like being on a ship for a long time. When you leave the ship and get back on land it takes a little getting used to. Also, driving a large motor home is not like driving a car. It takes a higher level of concentration and consideration of what is going on around you. Yet, even though I was tired, in my heart I knew the Lord wanted Kelly and I to be at that meeting. So, after a quick shave, shower and a change of clothes I was ready to go. We got there just as the meeting started.

My friend who invited Kelly and me to come was leading the praise and worship as she sang and played the guitar. There were about 40 people present for this informal fellowship. Kelly and I took a seat over to the side of the room and we joined in on the singing. We all sang and worshipped the Lord together for about 25 minutes. After that, my friend who was leading the singing sat down and said, "Well, I'm glad we are all here tonight. Does anyone have anything from the Lord that they would like to share?" A woman who was visiting from Tulsa, Oklahoma said, "Yes, I would like to share something. Last night I had a dream about mantles. I believe the Lord wants to do something tonight regarding mantles."

Then, another woman sitting on the other side of the room in response to the first comment said, "I just read a book by someone named Steven Brooks. He has written a book about mantles."

Then, one of the older men sitting in the room said, "I think the guy who wrote that book walked in tonight." Almost simultaneously, it seemed like the majority of the group at once said, "Ah, there's no way he would be here!"

Sitting over in the corner, I smiled, raised my hand and said, "Praise God, I'm here!" The whole room started laughing joyfully. It was an obvious set-up from the Lord. The man who saw me come into the meeting had previously read my book and had seen my picture on the back cover. He recognized me from my picture. The leader who was hosting the meeting looked at me with a big smile and said, "Well then, Steven, come on up here and teach us about mantles."

That night, I taught on the subject of mantles and then prayed and asked the Lord to release the mantles intended for those present in the meeting. Five people had there spiritual eyes opened by the Holy Spirit to see mantles falling through the roof of the building and coming to rest upon certain individuals. What a wonderful time we had in the Holy Spirit. And that, by the way, is how the Lord introduced me to the community of Moravian Falls. I've found that if you have a gifting from the Lord, then the Lord will promote you. There's no need to knock down doors and strain to try and make something happen. Your gifting will cause you to be found out.

## WE MUST COOPERATE

Even though mantles are being bestowed upon the Body of Christ to complete the assignments of Heaven, there still needs to be cooperation on our part. Often, before a mantle can be received, one needs to be taken off. We see this in the story of blind Bartimaeus. This man was blind and he sat by the side of the road and begged. When he heard that Jesus was passing by, he began to call out and say, "Jesus, Son of David, have mercy on me!" Even though the crowd around him tried to silence him, he kept speaking out louder than before. The statement *Son of David* was a testimony that this man believed Jesus was the Messiah. The scribes had taught that the Messiah would descend from David and that he would be identified as the *Son of David*. This was a declaration of faith.

Earlier in His ministry, Jesus went to minister in His hometown of Nazareth and there the people called Him the *Son of Mary* (see Mark 6). This was a derogatory title spoken on purpose to voice the mutual disrespect that the people of Nazareth had for Jesus. In Nazareth, Jesus marveled at the unbelief of the people and could not do any mighty works. But Bartimaeus was different. Jesus understood what the statement *Son of David* implied. This is why He stopped and called for Bartimaeus to come to Him.

It's very important to realize what Bartimaeus did when Jesus called for him. Let's look at it closely.

*And throwing aside his garment,* he rose and came to Jesus (Mark 10:50).

In Middle Eastern culture during the Lord's time on earth, a person who suffered a legitimate physical handicap was made to be identified in order to receive help. The culture of that time understood they had a moral and ethical obligation to help those who could not help themselves. The blind, lame, and incapacitated individuals were rendered aid by being given what was known as a *beggar's garment.* This garment identified them as being officially licensed to beg and of possessing a severe physical handicap.

What did blind Bartimaeus do with his beggar's garment when Jesus called for him? He threw it aside. In order to receive the new mantle that God has for you, you might have to first get rid of the old. Often this is easier said then done.

182

I can imagine many of the circumstances that could have surfaced when he decided to get rid of his garment. You have to understand that he was getting rid of his safety net; he was saying goodbye to his back-up plan. Somebody could have leaned over to him and said:

"Now hold on just a minute Bartimaeus. Let's not get too excited and emotionally carried away here. You've been sitting out here under the sun too long. You could be suffering from a heat stroke. It's affected your thinking."

Another could have said:

"Wait, Bartimaeus. What happens if it doesn't work? Why don't you roll up your garment and put it behind your back so Jesus won't see it? That way you will still have your garment incase this doesn't work out."

Or maybe someone said:

"Don't get rid of your garment. If you throw it away, you'll never find it again in this large crowd."

## GET RID OF THE BEGGARS' GARMENTS

My friends, you have to understand that Bartimaeus got rid of his garment while he was still blind. In order to receive the new and fresh anointing from God, it is often necessary to first throw off the old mantle. These old mantles often represent wrong ways of thinking. Get rid of any beggars' garments. Remove and abolish any excuse, any lie of the devil, that would suggest to you that you cannot have God's best. Strike from your mind such thoughts as:

"I could never afford to buy that."

"Sickness and disease run in my family and I'm next in line."

"I could never have a close walk with God because I'm not a preacher."

"I'm just a lowly worm and am unworthy of God's blessing."

Throw these wretched and polluted thoughts away. When Bartimaeus threw away his old beggar's garment, he knew that he would never be wearing that thing again. Right now, right where you are, just reach up to your shoulders and by faith pull off any old garments that need to be removed. The Holy Spirit is pinpointing those areas of your thoughts that need to have the slack removed. Don't settle for second best. Always hold out for God's best. Release your faith. Refuse to be held in bondage by only trusting in what you can see, feel, or logically explain. Step out on the Word of God and be led by the Holy Spirit. Your victory is assured. Praise the Lord for the new wardrobe you are receiving from Heaven. It's out with the old and in with the new. The time for a change of garments is now upon the Church.

We are standing on the edge of the greatest harvest of souls the world has ever seen. This is the most exciting time to be alive in the history of the world. We are going to see the Gospel preached throughout the entire world and then the end shall come (see Matt. 24:14). I want to be on the front line of what God is doing in the earth today. Don't you? Whatever mantle it is that God has for you, and whatever position it is that God has for you in the body of Christ, it is now time to rise up and seek the Lord like never before. God has something special for you and He will clothe you with fresh anointing, authority, and power by the Spirit of God.

# CHAPTER 12

# *Receive Your Mantle*

The final chapter in this book is purposely the shortest chapter. This is because asking and receiving from God is not complicated, nor is it necessary for it to be a long, drawn out process. "Faith comes by hearing, and hearing by the Word of God" (Rom. 10:17).

Now that you have built up your faith through the study of God's Word concerning mantles, as well as having looked at some of my personal testimonies and those of others, it is time for you to ask God for the mantle that He has for you. Some of the greatest answers I've had from *prayers of petition* occurred from short, specific requests that were made in confident faith to God. Please pray the following prayer from your heart in faith, knowing that God will answer your request.

"Dear Heavenly Father, I come to You in the name of Jesus. I ask unreservedly in faith for You to bestow upon my life the mantle that You have chosen for me. I ask You to reveal it to me by Your Spirit, and cause me to step into that which You have prepared for me to walk in. Thank You Father; I praise You for it. In Jesus name, Amen."

Now simply trust the Lord in His timing and in His method of delivery to get the chosen mantle to you. God will most assuredly answer your prayer. Thank God for it everyday, and your faith will become sight.

Recently, while at a minister's luncheon, I was asked by a certain minister how long I had sought the Lord before I received a heavenly mantle. My response was that I sought God regularly for two years before this experience took place in my life. Of course, that does not mean it would take that long for you. That was just my personal experience. My prayer is that you will receive your chosen mantle quickly, because I believe this has already been a deep desire within your heart and God has prepared your heart to receive. Whatever the time frame may be, just stay in faith and expectancy until you receive your heart's desire. Please meditate upon these following verses to strengthen your faith and to assure yourself that God will answer your prayer.

*Beloved, if our heart does not condemn us, we have confidence toward God. And* **whatever we ask** *we receive from*

*Him, because we keep His commandments and do those things that are pleasing in His sight* (1 John 3: 21-22).

*Now this is the confidence that we have in Him, that if* ***we ask anything according to His will,*** *He hears us. And if we know that He hears us,* ***whatever we ask,*** *we know that we have the petitions that we have asked of Him* (1 John 5:14-15).

In closing, I would like to share with you how suddenly and unexpectedly a new mantle can be transferred to you. A few years ago I went to a conference near Washington, DC, to see a fellow minister friend who was scheduled to speak. This conference was being held at a church and I had previously met the pastor. It was nice to catch up with my friend who was the guest speaker. After I finished speaking with him, I went over to visit the pastor who was also a friend of mine. As we were talking, he said, "There is someone here I would like for you to meet." He then introduced me to a very nice man named Wade Taylor. I had never met Wade before nor heard of him. Wade and I spoke briefly and as I was leaving, he said, "Next time you are in the Washington, DC, area, please give me a call."

Several months went by and my wife and I found ourselves in Northern Virginia, this time holding a meeting at a church that was very near to Washington, DC. After the meeting was over, we had a few days to relax before heading to our next ministry destination. Kelly said to me, "You know, we are very close to Washington, DC. Why don't you give Wade Taylor a call since he asked you to do so when we were in the area." Over the years, I've learned to listen to my wife. She often hears from the Lord concerning divine appointments and connections. I called Wade on the phone and told him I was close by and wanted to see if he would like to get together and get a bite to eat. He suggested that we meet the next day at a local restaurant that he was familiar with.

The next day, Kelly and I pulled up at the restaurant to meet Wade for lunch. We got there ten minutes early, but as we parked our car, we noticed Wade pull up at the same time and park right next to us. Kelly suggested to me that she would go inside and get a table while I would wait for him. As Kelly went to the restaurant, I went to Wade's car and waited for him to get out. As soon as he got out of the car the first thing he said was, "I want to tell you about three men who influenced my life and how their mantles were transferred to me." I thought to myself, "This is unusual. We haven't even gotten inside the restaurant yet and the conversation is already rolling." Those who know Wade know that this is not usually the way he acts. Wade is in his eighties and is quiet and reserved. He's a great Bible teacher, but when he is not ministering, he is low-key and prefers that others do the talking.

Now keep in mind that I had only met Wade one time before, and that only lasted about three minutes. As we took our seat at the table with Kelly, we continued our conversation. Wade shared about three men who have already gone on to be with the Lord who greatly influenced his life.

One of those men was John Wright Follette. John Follette was an anointed Bible teacher who lived a long life and graduated to Heaven in 1966. His teaching ministry took him around the world and his writings are still widely read today. John Follette was the type of man who would be considered a *mystic saint*. The phrase *mystic saint* implies someone who is deeply devoted to the Lord—a commitment going far beyond what most people would consider normal. This man devoted his whole life to the Lord by never marrying and by spending large amounts of time in prayer and study of God's Word. He lived in a very small home and had very little interest in material possessions. A relationship with the Lord such as this often forms an element of mystery around a person, because people tend to be intrigued by such an unusual type of consecration. Of course, you don't have to stay unmarried to have this type of walk with the Lord. We see in the Bible that Enoch developed a very deep walk with God *after* he had children, (see Gen. 5:22). Anyone can press into the same place of intimacy with the Lord if he or she is willing to sacrifice along the way.

Wade continued to tell me about John Follette's ministry by sharing stories about his life. Once John Follette preached a message while he was suspended in mid-air. He simply walked right off the platform as he was teaching and hovered in the air while he continued his message. After all, Peter walked on the water. There's not much difference between air or water. Both demonstrate the Holy Spirit's operation of the gift of the working of miracles mentioned by Paul in First Corinthians chapter 12. Wade went on to mention how John Follette often was a visiting teacher at a Bible College that he attended. As a student at the college, Wade loved John Follette's ministry.

One day he went by the room at the Bible College that John Follette was staying in. He went with the purpose of asking for the mantle. As he was invited in, they talked, and Wade took the opportunity to ask John Follette if he could have his mantle. The answer was "Yes," and that day John Follette laid his hands on Wade and transferred the mantle. What's interesting is that years later Wade went on to become the President of that Bible College!

Of course, at the restaurant table I'm wondering, "Why is he telling me all of this?" Wade went on to share with me the story of two other respected ministers that he was associated with and how similar mantles had been imparted to him. These two men also had very close walks with the Lord and had international ministries. Then, he relaxed and leaned back in his chair at the table and said, "Now, tell me about your ministry."

For about ten minutes I told about the ministry the Lord has given to me. I described how Kelly and I travel all over the country and to different parts of the world preaching and teaching the good news of Jesus Christ. I told about some of the great miracles that God has done in people's lives through our ministry. As we concluded our meal and our conversation, Wade said, "I believe we need to go outside and pray."

As we left the restaurant, we decided to sit in my car and pray there. I sat in the front driver's seat and Wade sat in the front passenger seat. Kelly graciously sat in the middle of the rear seat. To be honest, I wasn't sure what to pray about. I opened us up in prayer and tried praying for a few minutes but

I only felt like I was rambling. Not only did I feel like I was praying without a purpose but it seemed like Wade wasn't even paying attention. After two minutes of praying I decided to stop, so I wrapped up my prayer and said, "In Jesus name, amen." When I said that, Wade responded and said, "Good. Steven, I'll need your hands for this." I stretched out both of my hands and he grabbed them with his hands and held them. He then prayed and said, "Father, I now transfer the mantle of John Wright Follette, _____, _____ (he named the names of the other two ministers), and my mantle to Steven, now." He said, "Receive, receive."

I felt an impartation of the Holy Spirit as he prayed for me. It felt like a warm, liquid anointing that went from his hands into my hands and up my arms and rested on my shoulders. Then Wade did the most peculiar thing. He simply looked at Kelly and me and smiled and said, "Okay. Goodbye!" He then got out of the car and left. The whole incident to me was totally unexpected and rather unorthodox. I had to let Kelly drive home because I was inebriated in the Holy Spirit. After this took place I called my pastor friend who was good friends with Wade and I told him what happened. He said, "Steven, Wade only goes out when he is on divine assignments. He will only do what the Lord specifically directs him to do."

Since that day, Wade and I have become close friends. We have ministered in conferences together and have had late night conversations at his home, discussing the Lord and His goodness and glory. I was introduced to a deep well of spiritual truth through Wade and through studying the lives of the three ministers whose mantles he prayed for me to receive. Sometimes I think of how different my life would be if that event never took place. But the Lord wanted to add something to my life that expressed a beautiful facet of His nature that I had not had much exposure to. Walking with the Lord is exciting because you never know what a day may hold for you. There's nothing else like serving the Lord. Jesus is simply the best!

You may be wondering why I didn't share the names of the other two ministers. There are some secrets I keep to myself. At times I've spoken about them in meetings, but most often I just keep that hidden. Some things I like to treasure in my heart.

A mantle is an impartation of the Spirit of God. It's not only for increased empowerment, but it's also for increased revelation of the Lord. A fresh mantle, a fresh anointing, allows you to see the Lord in a new way that you've not seen Him in before. It's all about receiving more of the Lord into our lives. A person passing a mantle or releasing an impartation is only a vessel that the Lord flows through. We look to the Lord and worship Him, because God is the source of every anointing and gift that He graciously gives. As you worship the Lord and live your life fully for Him, every mantle, anointing, blessing, and gift from God will find its way to you.

# Prayer of Salvation and Holy Spirit Baptism

Perhaps you came across this book and have not yet had the opportunity to personally receive Jesus Christ as Savior and Lord. I would like to invite you to open your heart to Him now. Please read the following verses from the Bible out loud. When you read Bible verses out loud so that your physical ears can hear the Word of God, it allows faith to enter into your heart.

*And it shall come to pass that whoever calls on the name of the Lord shall be saved* (Acts 2:21).

*That if you confess with your mouth the Lord Jesus and believe in your heart that God has raised Him* [Jesus] *from the dead, you will be saved* (Romans 10:9).

*And do not be drunk with wine, in which is dissipation; but be filled with the Spirit* (Ephesians 5:18).

*And they were all filled with the Holy Spirit and began to speak with other tongues, as the Spirit gave them utterance* (Acts 2:4).

Now that you have read how you may be saved, you can obey the Word of God and make your life right with God. Simply pray the following prayer from your heart and Jesus will give you His eternal life.

"Dear Lord Jesus, I confess that you are the Son of God. I believe that you were raised from the dead and are alive forevermore. Please come into my heart and forgive me of all my sins. I turn away from all sin and I give my life completely to you. Please fill me with your precious Holy Spirit so that I may speak in tongues and worship you all the days of my life. Thank you Jesus for saving me and for filling me with your Holy Spirit. I love you!"

Now lift your hands and begin to praise God for saving you. Open your mouth and begin to speak in the new heavenly language that the Holy Spirit has given you. Let the new words and syllables come forth, not your own language, but the language the Holy Spirit gives you. Don't be concerned about how it sounds. It might not make sense to your mind, but it is your spirit communicating with God, and God understands everything you are speaking.

Praise the Lord! You are now a Spirit-filled Christian on your way to Heaven. Every day, speak in tongues to glorify God and to strengthen yourself. You will be refreshed as you do.

Now that you belong to Jesus, ask your heavenly Father to help you find a new church home so that you can grow spiritually and continue your walk with God. The Holy Spirit will lead you as you search for the Christian church that God wants you to be a part of. Look for a church where you can sense the love of God and where people take a genuine interest in you. Seek out a church that believes the whole Bible and preaches it without compromise. And always remember that *God loves you*.

# Partner Information

The ministry of Steven Brooks is touching lives around the world. Partnering with Brother Steven to help spread the Gospel is a great opportunity to be a part of the end-time move of God's Holy Spirit. Steven Brooks is committed to go anywhere God sends him and to preach and demonstrate the miracle working power of God. When you partner with Brother Steven, you partner with a minister who has surrendered his life for the purpose of serving God both day and night. Would you like to be a part of helping Steven spread the fires of revival all across America and the nations of the world? Because of the high value that God places upon ministry partnership, Steven views each partner as someone who is divinely sent from God. Here are the benefits you receive as a partner with this ministry.

- Impartation that is upon Steven's life to be upon you to help you accomplish what God has called you to do.

- Consistent prayer for you by Brother Steven.

- Monthly partner newsletter to build your faith and feed your spirit.

- Believe God for His best return on all your giving.

- Eternal share in the heavenly rewards obtained through this ministry.

As a partner with this ministry, your responsibilities are to:

- Pray for Brother Steven, his family, and his ministry on a regular basis.

- Support the ministry with a monthly financial contribution.

To join with Brother Steven in ministry partnership and become a part of preaching the Gospel around the world, simply visit our website at www.stevenbrooks.org and click on the "Partner" link and sign up. Or write to us and please include the necessary information below so that we can register you as a ministry partner. We look forward to hearing from you and we thank God for your commitment as a ministry partner!

- Name
- Address
- City

- State
- Zip Code
- Country
- E-mail Address

For booking information and upcoming meetings

*Please visit our Website at:*
www.stevenbrooks.org

*or e-mail us at:*
info@stevenbrooks.org.

# *About the Author*

Steven Brooks is a dynamic preacher of the Gospel whose ministry is one of crystal clear preaching followed by unusual signs and wonders. He operates in a powerful apostolic-prophetic ministry that is coupled with a Heaven sent gift of divine healing. As the supernatural gifts of "special faith" and the "working of miracles" operate in his ministry, remarkable miracles take place.

All types of sicknesses and diseases are healed as Steven prays for the sick. From incurable cases that doctors have completely given up on to mental disorders, countless numbers of people have been healed by the power of God. Even broken bones have been healed instantly, along with severe cases of back conditions such as scoliosis of the spine and injuries suffered through traumatic car accidents. Precious people suffering from cancer, cysts, tumors, hernias, and other physical maladies have received miracles of healing through Steven's ministry.

As Steven prays for the sick, words of knowledge and prophecy begin to flow as the spirit of prophecy comes upon him. His joyful attitude has blessed the hearts of multitudes through his ministering in conferences, churches, crusades, and radio and television appearances.

Steven's meetings are always exciting to be in because of his desire to see Jesus lifted up and because of his sensitivity to the Holy Spirit. Today, Steven and his family travel extensively throughout America and the world preaching the Gospel of the Lord Jesus Christ. Steven and his wife, Kelly, presently reside in Moravian Falls, North Carolina and have three children, Matthew, Jennifer, and Abigail.